Super Easy

MEDITERRANEAN DIET

Cookbook for Beginners 2023

Simple and Nutritious Mediterranean Recipes to Kickstart a Healthy Eating Journey with a 28-Day Meal Plan to Transform Your Eating Habits

Reece Lambert

All Rights Reserved.

The content contained within this book may not be reproduced, duplicated, or transmitted without direct written permission from the author or the publisher. Under no circumstances will any blame or legal responsibility be held against the publisher, or author, for any damages, reparation, or monetary loss due to the information contained within this book, either directly or indirectly.

Legal Notice: This book is copyright protected. It is only for personal use. You cannot amend, distribute, sell, use, quote or paraphrase any part, or the content within this book, without the consent of the author or publisher.

Disclaimer Notice:

Please note the information contained within this document is for educational and entertainment purposes only. All effort has been executed to present accurate, up to date, reliable, complete information. No warranties of any kind are declared or implied. Readers acknowledge that the author is not engaged in the rendering of legal, financial, medical, or professional advice. The content within this book has been derived from various sources. Please consult a licensed professional before attempting any techniques outlined in this book. By reading this document, the reader agrees that under no circumstances is the author responsible for any losses, direct or indirect, that are incurred as a result of the use of the information contained within this document, including, but not limited to, errors, omissions, or inaccuracies.

CONTENTS

INTRODUCTION I
Characteristics of the Mediterranean Diet I
What are the effects of the Mediterranean Diet on people's life and health? III
Some questions and answers about the Mediterranean Diet V

28-Day Meal Plan VI

Measurement Conversions VIII

Breakfast Recipes 6
Almond-cherry Oatmeal Bowls 6
Parmesan Oatmeal With Greens 6
Red Pepper Coques With Pine Nuts 7
Dilly Salmon Frittata 7
Apple & Date Smoothie 8
Spicy Tofu Tacos With Cherry Tomato Salsa 8
Chia & Almond Oatmeal 9
Mushroom And Caramelized Onion Musakhan 9
Chocolate-strawberry Smoothie 10
Roasted Vegetable Panini 10
Banana & Chocolate Porridge 11
Pumpkin-yogurt Parfaits 11
Quick & Easy Bread In A Mug 11
Mango-yogurt Smoothie 12
White Pizzas With Arugula And Spinach 12
Maple Berry & Walnut Oatmeal 13
Honey & Feta Frozen Yogurt 13
Kale And Apple Smoothie 13
Cherry Tomato & Mushroom Frittata 14
Savory Breakfast Oatmeal 14
Crustless Tiropita (greek Cheese Pie) 15
Egg Bake 15
Energy Nut Smoothie 16
Basil Scrambled Eggs 16
Easy Alfalfa Sprout And Nut Rolls 17
Tomato And Egg Scramble 17

Beans, Grains, And Pastas Recipes 18

- Slow Cooker Pork & Bean Cassoulet 18
- Veggie & Egg Quinoa With Pancetta 18
- Swiss Chard Couscous With Feta Cheese 19
- Smoky Paprika Chickpeas 19
- Lemony Tuna Barley With Capers 19
- Rosemary Barley With Walnuts 20
- Black Bean & Chickpea Burgers 20
- Two-bean Cassoulet 21
- Fofu Spaghetti Bolognese 21
- Autumn Vegetable & Rigatoni Bake 22
- Turkish-style Orzo 22
- Mushroom & Green Onion Rice Pilaf 22
- Slow Cooked Turkey And Brown Rice 23
- Vegetable Quinoa & Garbanzo Skillet 23
- Creamy Asparagus & Parmesan Linguine 24
- Simple Green Rice 24
- Cherry, Apricot, And Pecan Brown Rice Bowl 25
- Paprika Spinach & Chickpea Bowl 25
- Asparagus & Goat Cheese Rice Salad 26
- Swoodles With Almond Butter Sauce 26
- Chili Pork Rice 27
- Creamy Shrimp With Tie Pasta 27
- Lemon-basil Spaghetti 28
- Carrot & Caper Chickpeas 28
- Hearty Butternut Spinach, And Cheeses Lasagna 29
- Bean And Veggie Pasta 29

Fish And Seafood Recipes 30

- Avocado Shrimp Ceviche 30
- Crab Stuffed Celery Sticks 30
- Baked Salmon With Tarragon Mustard Sauce 31
- Cod Fillets In Mushroom Sauce 31
- Leek & Olive Cod Casserole 32
- Baked Halibut Steaks With Vegetables 32
- Grilled Lemon Pesto Salmon 33
- Caper & Herring Stuffed Eggs 33
- Calamari In Garlic-cilantro Sauce 33
- Seafood Stew 34
- Seared Halibut With Moroccan Chermoula 34
- Lemony Sea Bass 35
- Spicy Grilled Shrimp With Lemon Wedges 35
- Dill Chutney Salmon 36
- Cheesy Smoked Salmon Crostini 36
- Roasted Cod With Cabbage 36
- Baked Cod With Vegetables 37
- One-skillet Salmon With Olives & Escarole 37

Herby Cod Skewers	38
Pan-seared Trout With Tzatziki	38
Drunken Mussels With Lemon-butter Sauce	38
Parchment Orange & Dill Salmon	39
Sole Piccata With Capers	39
Rosemary Wine Poached Haddock	39
Garlic Shrimp With Arugula Pesto	40
Garlic Shrimp With Mushrooms	40

Sides, Salads, And Soups Recipes 41

Sumptuous Greek Vegetable Salad	41
Cucumber & Spelt Salad With Chicken	41
Ritzy Summer Fruit Salad	42
Chili Lentil Soup	42
Root Vegetable Roast	43
Arugula & Caper Green Salad	43
Collard Green & Rice Salad	43
Tri-color Salad	44
Spinach & Chickpea Soup With Sausages	44
Zesty Asparagus Salad	44
Feta & Cannellini Bean Soup	45
Corn & Cucumber Salad	45
Simple Tuna Salad	46
Herby Yogurt Sauce	46
Bell Pepper & Roasted Cabbage Salad	46
Arugula & Fruit Salad	47
Leek Cream Soup With Hazelnuts	47
Italian Pork Meatball Soup	47
Mushroom And Soba Noodle Soup	48
Minty Bulgur With Fried Halloumi	48
Fruit Salad With Sesame Seeds & Nuts	49
Sautéed Kale With Olives	49
Cheese & Pecan Salad With Orange Dressing	50
Bean & Squash Soup	50
Picante Avocado Salad With Anchovies	51
Cabbage & Turkey Soup	51

Vegetable Mains And Meatless Recipes 52

Brussels Sprouts Linguine	52
Artichoke & Bean Pot	52
Veggie Rice Bowls With Pesto Sauce	53
Spicy Kale With Almonds	53
Veggie-stuffed Portabello Mushrooms	54
Baked Potato With Veggie Mix	54
Grilled Vegetable Skewers	55
Grilled Za´atar Zucchini Rounds	55
Chili Vegetable Skillet	56

Cauliflower Hash With Carrots ... 56
Garlicky Broccoli Rabe ... 57
Cauliflower Rice Risotto With Mushrooms ... 57
Chickpea Lettuce Wraps With Celery ... 57
Eggplant Rolls In Tomato Sauce ... 58
Roasted Vegetable Medley ... 58
Chargrilled Vegetable Kebabs ... 59
Italian Hot Green Beans ... 59
Celery And Mustard Greens ... 60
Easy Zucchini Patties ... 60
Simple Oven-baked Green Beans ... 60
Homemade Vegetarian Moussaka ... 61
Pea & Carrot Noodles ... 61
Grilled Eggplant "steaks" With Sauce ... 62
Cauliflower Cakes With Goat Cheese ... 62
Ratatouille ... 63
Tahini & Feta Butternut Squash ... 63

Poultry And Meats Recipes ... 64

Rosemary Pork Chops With Cabbage Mix ... 64
Herby Beef Soup ... 64
Chicken Sausage & Zucchini Soup ... 65
Chicken Thighs With Roasted Artichokes ... 65
Mushroom Chicken Piccata ... 66
Apricot Chicken Rice Bowls ... 66
Spanish Chicken Skillet ... 67
Baked Beef With Kale Slaw & Bell Peppers ... 67
Roasted Pork Tenderloin With Apple Sauce ... 68
Turmeric Green Bean & Chicken Bake ... 68
Marjoram Pork Loin With Ricotta Cheese ... 68
Mushroom & Pork Stew ... 69
Rosemary Spatchcock Chicken ... 69
Beef Stuffed Peppers ... 70
Valencian Arroz Con Pollo ... 70
Juicy Almond Turkey ... 71
Lamb Kebabs With Lemon-yogurt Sauce ... 71
Holiday Leg Of Lamb ... 71
Pork Tenderloin With Caraway Seeds ... 72
Chicken Tagine With Vegetables ... 72
Chicken Meatballs With Peach Topping ... 73
Grilled Chicken And Zucchini Kebabs ... 73
Original Meatballs ... 74
Baked Teriyaki Turkey Meatballs ... 74
Pork Chops In Tomato Olive Sauce ... 75
One-pan Turkish Turkey ... 75

Fruits, Desserts And Snacks Recipes ... 76

- Roasted Eggplant Hummus ... 76
- Artichoke & Curly Kale Flatbread ... 76
- Speedy Cucumber Canapes ... 77
- Basic Pudding With Kiwi ... 77
- Iberian Spread For Sandwiches ... 77
- Cheese Stuffed Potato Skins ... 78
- Spicy Roasted Chickpeas ... 78
- Garbanzo Patties With Cilantro-yogurt Sauce ... 79
- Tuna, Tomato & Burrata Salad ... 79
- White Bean Dip With Pita Wedges ... 79
- Sicilian Almond Granita ... 80
- Pepperoni Fat Head Pizza ... 80
- Berry And Rhubarb Cobbler ... 81
- Homemade Studentenfutter ... 81
- Home-style Trail Mix ... 82
- Fig & Mascarpone Toasts With Pistachios ... 82
- Coconut Blueberries With Brown Rice ... 82
- Authentic Greek Potato Skins ... 83
- Amaretto Nut Bars ... 83
- Quick & Easy Red Dip ... 83
- Apple And Berries Ambrosia ... 84
- Pecan & Raspberry & Frozen Yogurt Cups ... 84
- Portuguese Orange Mug Cake ... 84
- Cinnamon Pear & Oat Crisp With Pecans ... 85
- Dates Stuffed With Mascarpone & Almonds ... 85
- Chocolate And Avocado Mousse ... 85

Appendix : Recipes Index ... 86

INTRODUCTION

Welcome to Reece Lambert's Mediterranean Diet Cookbook, an odyssey through the rich tapestry of a region known as much for its storied history as for its culinary prowess.

Reece Lambert doesn't just present you with a set of recipes; he beckons you into a world where each dish carries with it tales of generations, traditions passed down through time, and a deep reverence for the land and sea.

But why the Mediterranean? The Mediterranean Diet isn't just a passing culinary trend. It's a testament to a region's capacity to harness the bounty of its surroundings, to take sun-ripened tomatoes, fresh-caught fish, heart-healthy olives, and aromatic herbs and create meals that nourish the soul as much as the body. Renowned for its numerous health benefits—from heart health to cognitive well-being, from weight management to improved digestion—the Mediterranean Diet offers a sustainable and flavorful approach to eating well.

So, as you turn these pages, picture yourself on a sun-drenched terrace overlooking the sea and the promise of a meal that's both hearty and healthy. Let Reece Lambert be your guide on this culinary voyage, one where every dish is a destination, and every bite, a journey.

Dive in, embrace the Mediterranean spirit, and let's celebrate the harmony of taste and wellness. Welcome to a world of gastronomic wonder.

Characteristics of the Mediterranean Diet

Whole Grains: Consumption of whole grains like whole wheat, barley, millet, oats, and brown rice is encouraged.

Fresh Vegetables and Fruits: A high intake of diverse vegetables and fruits is a hallmark. Common choices include olives, tomatoes, eggplants, cucumbers, and citrus fruits.

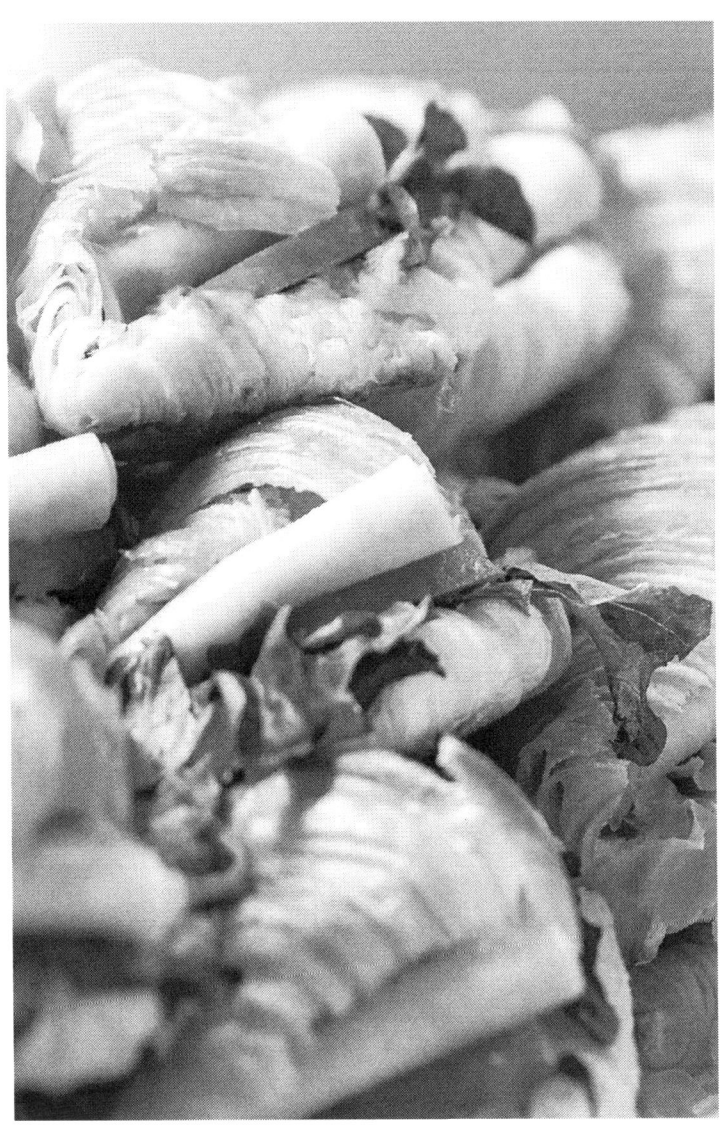

Healthy Fats: The diet is rich in healthy fats, especially from olive oil, which is used abundantly in cooking and dressings. Nuts and seeds are also sources of healthy fats and are consumed regularly.

Legumes: Beans, lentils, chickpeas, and other legumes are integral protein sources and are eaten regularly.

Fish and Seafood: There's a preference for fish and seafood over red meat. Fish like sardines, mackerel, and salmon, which are rich in omega-3 fatty acids, are commonly eaten.

Moderate Dairy Intake: Dairy, especially cheese and yogurt, is consumed in moderation. Options like feta and Greek yogurt are popular choices.

Limited Red Meat: Red meat is consumed less frequently, often only a few times a month.

Wine: Moderate consumption of red wine is common, often enjoyed with meals. However, this is optional and should be in moderation.

Herbs and Spices: Instead of salt, herbs and spices like basil, oregano, rosemary, and garlic are used to flavor dishes, offering both taste and health benefits.

Physical Activity: A Mediterranean lifestyle emphasizes the importance of regular physical activity.

Social Dining: Meals are often seen as a social event, meant to be enjoyed with family and friends. This communal aspect contributes to overall well-being.

Limited Processed Foods: Minimal consumption of processed foods and added sugars. The focus is on fresh, seasonal, and locally-sourced foods.

Eggs and Poultry: These are consumed in moderation, more often than red meat but less frequently than fish.

The Mediterranean Diet isn't just about food—it encompasses a holistic approach to life, emphasizing the importance of community, physical activity, and savoring every bite. Numerous studies suggest that it can contribute to heart health, weight management, and even longevity.

What are the effects of the Mediterranean Diet on people's life and health?

The Mediterranean Diet is widely researched and has been shown to have a variety of beneficial effects on health and overall well-being. Heart Health: One of the most recognized benefits of the Mediterranean Diet is its positive impact on cardiovascular health. It has been linked to reduced risks of coronary heart disease, myocardial infarction (heart attack), and ischemic stroke.

- **Weight Management**

The diet promotes a balanced and sustainable way of eating, which can assist in weight loss and maintaining a healthy weight.

- **Blood Sugar and Diabetes**

Adherence to the Mediterranean Diet has been associated with improved blood sugar control and a reduced risk of type 2 diabetes.

- **Reduced Cancer Risk**

Some studies have suggested that the Mediterranean Diet may lower the risk of certain cancers, especially colorectal, breast, and prostate cancers.

- **Brain Health**

There's evidence suggesting that the diet can reduce the risk of neurodegenerative diseases like Alzheimer's and Parkinson's. It may also improve cognitive function in the elderly.

- **Mood and Mental Health**

Some research indicates a potential protective effect against depression and anxiety. The omega-3 fatty acids from fish, combined with other nutrients in the diet, may support brain health and mood regulation.

- **Longevity**

The Mediterranean Diet might play a role in promoting longer life. This is likely due to the combined effects of reduced risks of chronic diseases and its emphasis on quality whole foods.

- **Improved Digestive Health**

The high fiber content from whole grains, fruits, and vegetables supports healthy digestion and may reduce the risk of gastrointestinal diseases.

- **Reduced Inflammation**

The diet's emphasis on anti-inflammatory foods, like olive oil and nuts, can lead to reduced markers of inflammation in the body.

- **Bone Health**

Some elements of the diet, like olive oil and fish, have been linked to better bone density and reduced risk of osteoporosis.

- **Improved Rheumatoid Arthritis Symptoms**

Early research suggests that the diet might help alleviate some symptoms of rheumatoid arthritis due to its anti-inflammatory properties.

- **Better Kidney Health**

Preliminary studies indicate potential protective effects against chronic kidney disease.

- **Holistic Well-being**

The Mediterranean lifestyle, which encompasses shared meals, physical activity, and a slower pace of life, contributes to improved mental well-being and quality of life.

It's important to note that while the Mediterranean Diet offers numerous health benefits, it's most effective when viewed as part of a holistic lifestyle, including regular physical activity, adequate sleep, stress management, and avoiding smoking and excessive alcohol consumption.

Some questions and answers about the Mediterranean Diet

Q: What is the Mediterranean Diet based on?

A: The Mediterranean Diet is based on the traditional eating patterns of countries bordering the Mediterranean Sea, like Italy, Greece, and Spain. It emphasizes whole foods, healthy fats, lean proteins, and a balanced lifestyle.

Q: Why is olive oil so essential in the Mediterranean Diet?

A: Olive oil, especially extra-virgin olive oil, is a primary source of healthy monounsaturated fats. It's rich in antioxidants and anti-inflammatory compounds, promoting heart health and overall well-being.

Q: Are all fats accepted in this diet?

A: No. While the Mediterranean Diet emphasizes healthy fats from sources like olive oil, nuts, and fish, it recommends limiting saturated fats and avoiding trans fats.

Q: How does the Mediterranean Diet affect heart health?

A: The diet is known to reduce risks of heart diseases by improving cholesterol levels, reducing blood pressure, and decreasing inflammation, among other benefits.

Q: Is red wine allowed in the Mediterranean Diet?

A: Yes, in moderation. While red wine is commonly consumed, it's usually in moderate amounts and often enjoyed with meals. If one doesn't drink, it's not recommended to start.

Q: How does the diet impact weight management?

A: The Mediterranean Diet promotes a balanced and sustainable way of eating. The high fiber content and healthy fats can lead to feeling fuller and can assist in weight loss and maintenance.

Q: Is the Mediterranean Diet vegetarian?

A: While it's rich in plant-based foods, it's not strictly vegetarian. It includes fish, poultry, and occasionally red meat. However, it can be easily adapted to a vegetarian or vegan lifestyle.

Q: How is the Mediterranean Diet different from a low-carb diet?

A: While both diets emphasize whole foods and healthy fats, the Mediterranean Diet includes a variety of carbohydrates like whole grains, fruits, and legumes, making it not strictly low-carb.

Q: Why is the social aspect emphasized in the Mediterranean Diet?

A: Meals in Mediterranean cultures are often social events, meant to be enjoyed with family and friends. This communal aspect contributes to mental well-being and a holistic approach to health.

28-Day Meal Plan

Day	Breakfast	Lunch	Dinner
1	Almond-cherry Oatmeal Bowls 6	Slow Cooker Pork & Bean Cassoulet 18	Sumptuous Greek Vegetable Salad 41
2	Parmesan Oatmeal With Greens 6	Black Bean & Chickpea Burgers 20	Cucumber & Spelt Salad With Chicken 41
3	Red Pepper Coques With Pine Nuts 7	Fofu Spaghetti Bolognese 21	Ritzy Summer Fruit Salad 42
4	Dilly Salmon Frittata 7	Autumn Vegetable & Rigatoni Bake 22	Chili Lentil Soup 42
5	Apple & Date Smoothie 8	Mushroom & Green Onion Rice Pilaf 22	Root Vegetable Roast 43
6	Spicy Tofu Tacos With Cherry Tomato Salsa 8	Slow Cooked Turkey And Brown Rice 23	Arugula & Caper Green Salad 43
7	Chia & Almond Oatmeal 9	Bean And Veggie Pasta 29	Collard Green & Rice Salad 43
8	Mushroom And Caramelized Onion Musakhan 9	Avocado Shrimp Ceviche 30	Tri-color Salad 44
9	Chocolate-strawberry Smoothie 10	Cod Fillets In Mushroom Sauce 31	Spinach & Chickpea Soup With Sausages 44
10	Roasted Vegetable Panini 10	Leek & Olive Cod Casserole 32	Zesty Asparagus Salad 44
11	Banana & Chocolate Porridge 11	Baked Halibut Steaks With Vegetables 32	Feta & Cannellini Bean Soup 45
12	Pumpkin-yogurt Parfaits 11	Grilled Lemon Pesto Salmon 33	Corn & Cucumber Salad 45
13	Quick & Easy Bread In A Mug 11	Seafood Stew 34	Simple Tuna Salad 46
14	Mango-yogurt Smoothie 12	Seared Halibut With Moroccan Chermoula 34	Herby Yogurt Sauce 46

Day	Breakfast	Lunch	Dinner
15	White Pizzas With Arugula And Spinach 12	Lemony Sea Bass 35	Bell Pepper & Roasted Cabbage Salad 46
16	Maple Berry & Walnut Oatmeal 13	Rosemary Pork Chops With Cabbage Mix 64	Arugula & Fruit Salad 47
17	Honey & Feta Frozen Yogurt 13	Chicken Sausage & Zucchini Soup 65	Leek Cream Soup With Hazelnuts 47
18	Kale And Apple Smoothie 13	Chicken Thighs With Roasted Artichokes 65	Italian Pork Meatball Soup 47
19	Cherry Tomato & Mushroom Frittata 14	Mushroom Chicken Piccata 66	Mushroom And Soba Noodle Soup 48
20	Savory Breakfast Oatmeal 14	Apricot Chicken Rice Bowls 66	Minty Bulgur With Fried Halloumi 48
21	Crustless Tiropita (greek Cheese Pie) 15	Spanish Chicken Skillet 67	Fruit Salad With Sesame Seeds & Nuts 49
22	Egg Bake 15	Baked Beef With Kale Slaw & Bell Peppers 67	Sautéed Kale With Olives 49
23	Energy Nut Smoothie 16	Roasted Pork Tenderloin With Apple Sauce 67	Cheese & Pecan Salad With Orange Dressing 50
24	Basil Scrambled Eggs 16	Turmeric Green Bean & Chicken Bake 68	Bean & Squash Soup 50
25	Easy Alfalfa Sprout And Nut Rolls 17	Marjoram Pork Loin With Ricotta Cheese 68	Picante Avocado Salad With Anchovies 51
26	Tomato And Egg Scramble 17	Mushroom & Pork Stew 69	Cabbage & Turkey Soup 51
27	Veggie & Egg Quinoa With Pancetta 18	Rosemary Spatchcock Chicken 69	Brussels Sprouts Linguine 52
28	Swiss Chard Couscous With Feta Cheese 19	Beef Stuffed Peppers 70	Artichoke & Bean Pot 52

Measurement Conversions

BASIC KITCHEN CONVERSIONS & EQUIVALENTS

DRY MEASUREMENTS CONVERSION CHART

3 TEASPOONS = 1 TABLESPOON = 1/16 CUP

6 TEASPOONS = 2 TABLESPOONS = 1/8 CUP

12 TEASPOONS = 4 TABLESPOONS = 1/4 CUP

24 TEASPOONS = 8 TABLESPOONS = 1/2 CUP

36 TEASPOONS = 12 TABLESPOONS = 3/4 CUP

48 TEASPOONS = 16 TABLESPOONS = 1 CUP

METRIC TO US COOKING CONVERSIONS

OVEN TEMPERATURES

120 °C = 250 °F

160 °C = 320 °F

180° C = 350 °F

205 °C = 400 °F

220 °C = 425 °F

LIQUID MEASUREMENTS CONVERSION CHART

8 FLUID OUNCES = 1 CUP = 1/2 PINT = 1/4 QUART

16 FLUID OUNCES = 2 CUPS = 1 PINT = 1/2 QUART

32 FLUID OUNCES = 4 CUPS = 2 PINTS = 1 QUART

= 1/4 GALLON

128 FLUID OUNCES = 16 CUPS = 8 PINTS = 4 QUARTS = 1 GALLON

BAKING IN GRAMS

1 CUP FLOUR = 140 GRAMS

1 CUP SUGAR = 150 GRAMS

1 CUP POWDERED SUGAR = 160 GRAMS

1 CUP HEAVY CREAM = 235 GRAMS

VOLUME

1 MILLILITER = 1/5 TEASPOON

5 ML = 1 TEASPOON

15 ML = 1 TABLESPOON

240 ML = 1 CUP OR 8 FLUID OUNCES

1 LITER = 34 FL. OUNCES

WEIGHT

1 GRAM = .035 OUNCES

100 GRAMS = 3.5 OUNCES

500 GRAMS = 1.1 POUNDS

1 KILOGRAM = 35 OUNCES

US TO METRIC COOKING CONVERSIONS

1/5 TSP = 1 ML

1 TSP = 5 ML

1 TBSP = 15 ML

1 FL OUNCE = 30 ML

1 CUP = 237 ML

1 PINT (2 CUPS) = 473 ML

1 QUART (4 CUPS) = .95 LITER

1 GALLON (16 CUPS) = 3.8 LITERS

1 OZ = 28 GRAMS

1 POUND = 454 GRAMS

BUTTER

1 CUP BUTTER = 2 STICKS = 8 OUNCES = 230 GRAMS = 8 TABLESPOONS

WHAT DOES 1 CUP EQUAL

1 CUP = 8 FLUID OUNCES

1 CUP = 16 TABLESPOONS

1 CUP = 48 TEASPOONS

1 CUP = 1/2 PINT

1 CUP = 1/4 QUART

1 CUP = 1/16 GALLON

1 CUP = 240 ML

BAKING PAN CONVERSIONS

1 CUP ALL-PURPOSE FLOUR = 4.5 OZ

1 CUP ROLLED OATS = 3 OZ 1 LARGE EGG = 1.7 OZ

1 CUP BUTTER = 8 OZ 1 CUP MILK = 8 OZ

1 CUP HEAVY CREAM = 8.4 OZ

1 CUP GRANULATED SUGAR = 7.1 OZ

1 CUP PACKED BROWN SUGAR = 7.75 OZ

1 CUP VEGETABLE OIL = 7.7 OZ

1 CUP UNSIFTED POWDERED SUGAR = 4.4 OZ

BAKING PAN CONVERSIONS

9-INCH ROUND CAKE PAN = 12 CUPS

10-INCH TUBE PAN = 16 CUPS

11-INCH BUNDT PAN = 12 CUPS

9-INCH SPRINGFORM PAN = 10 CUPS

9 X 5 INCH LOAF PAN = 8 CUPS

9-INCH SQUARE PAN = 8 CUPS

Breakfast Recipes

Almond-cherry Oatmeal Bowls

Servings: 2
Cooking Time: 45 Minutes

Ingredients:

- ½ cup old-fashioned oats
- ¾ cup almond milk
- ½ tsp almond extract
- ½ tsp vanilla
- 1 egg, beaten
- 2 tbsp maple syrup
- ½ cup dried cherries, chopped
- 2 tbsp slivered raw almonds

Directions:

1. In a microwave-safe bowl, combine oats, almond milk, almond extract, vanilla, egg, and maple syrup and mix well.
2. Microwave for 5-6 minutes, stirring every 2 minutes until oats are soft. Spoon the mixture into 2 bowls. Top with cherries and almonds and serve. Enjoy!

Nutrition Info:

- Info Per Serving: Calories: 287; Fat: 9g; Protein: 11g; Carbs: 43g.

Parmesan Oatmeal With Greens

Servings: 2
Cooking Time: 18 Minutes

Ingredients:

- 1 tablespoon olive oil
- ¼ cup minced onion
- 2 cups greens (arugula, baby spinach, chopped kale, or Swiss chard)
- ¾ cup gluten-free old-fashioned oats
- 1½ cups water, or low-sodium chicken stock
- 2 tablespoons Parmesan cheese
- Salt, to taste
- Pinch freshly ground black pepper

Directions:

1. Heat the olive oil in a saucepan over medium-high heat. Add the minced onion and sauté for 2 minutes, or until softened.
2. Add the greens and stir until they begin to wilt. Transfer this mixture to a bowl and set aside.
3. Add the oats to the pan and let them toast for about 2 minutes. Add the water and bring the oats to a boil.
4. Reduce the heat to low, cover, and let the oats cook for 10 minutes, or until the liquid is absorbed and the oats are tender.
5. Stir the Parmesan cheese into the oats, and add the onion and greens back to the pan. Add additional water if needed, so the oats are creamy and not dry.
6. Stir well and season with salt and black pepper to taste. Serve warm.

Nutrition Info:

- Info Per Serving: Calories: 257; Fat: 14.0g; Protein: 12.2g; Carbs: 30.2g.

Red Pepper Coques With Pine Nuts

Servings: 4
Cooking Time: 45 Minutes

Ingredients:

- Dough:
- 3 cups almond flour
- ½ teaspoon instant or rapid-rise yeast
- 2 teaspoons raw honey
- 1⅓ cups ice water
- 3 tablespoons extra-virgin olive oil
- 1½ teaspoons sea salt
- Red Pepper Topping:
- 4 tablespoons extra-virgin olive oil, divided
- 2 cups jarred roasted red peppers, patted dry and sliced thinly
- 2 large onions, halved and sliced thin
- 3 garlic cloves, minced
- ¼ teaspoon red pepper flakes
- 2 bay leaves
- 3 tablespoons maple syrup
- 1½ teaspoons sea salt
- 3 tablespoons red whine vinegar
- For Garnish:
- ¼ cup pine nuts (optional)
- 1 tablespoon minced fresh parsley

Directions:

1. Make the Dough:
2. Combine the flour, yeast, and honey in a food processor, pulse to combine well. Gently add water while pulsing. Let the dough sit for 10 minutes.
3. Mix the olive oil and salt in the dough and knead the dough until smooth. Wrap in plastic and refrigerate for at least 1 day.
4. Make the Topping:
5. Heat 1 tablespoon of olive oil in a nonstick skillet over medium heat until shimmering.
6. Add the red peppers, onions, garlic, red pepper flakes, bay leaves, maple syrup, and salt. Sauté for 20 minutes or until the onion is caramelized.
7. Turn off the heat and discard the bay leaves. Remove the onion from the skillet and baste with wine vinegar. Let them sit until ready to use.
8. Make the Coques:
9. Preheat the oven to 500ºF. Grease two baking sheets with 1 tablespoon of olive oil.
10. Divide the dough ball into four balls, then press and shape them into equal-sized oval. Arrange the ovals on the baking sheets and pierce each dough about 12 times.
11. Rub the ovals with 2 tablespoons of olive oil and bake for 7 minutes or until puffed. Flip the ovals halfway through the cooking time.
12. Spread the ovals with the topping and pine nuts, then bake for an additional 15 minutes or until well browned.
13. Remove the coques from the oven and spread with parsley. Allow to cool for 10 minutes before serving.

Nutrition Info:

- Info Per Serving: Calories: 658;Fat: 23.1g;Protein: 3.4g;Carbs: 112.0g.

Dilly Salmon Frittata

Servings: 4
Cooking Time: 35 Minutes

Ingredients:

- 2 tbsp olive oil
- 1 cup cream cheese
- 1 cup smoked salmon, chopped
- 8 eggs, whisked
- 1 tsp dill, chopped
- 2 tbsp milk
- Salt and black pepper to taste

Directions:

1. Preheat oven to 360 F. In a bowl, place all the ingredients and stir to combine. Warm olive oil in a pan over medium heat and pour in the mixture. Cook until the base is set, about 3-4 minutes. Place the pan in the oven and bake until the top is golden, about 5 minutes. Serve sliced into wedges.

Nutrition Info:

- Info Per Serving: Calories: 418;Fat: 37g;Protein: 19.6g;Carbs: 3g.

Apple & Date Smoothie

Servings: 1
Cooking Time: 5 Minutes

Ingredients:
- 1 apple, peeled and chopped
- ½ cup milk
- 4 dates
- 1 tsp ground cinnamon

Directions:
1. In a blender, place the milk, ½ cup of water, dates, cinnamon, and apple. Blitz until smooth. Let chill in the fridge for 30 minutes. Serve in a tall glass.

Nutrition Info:
- Info Per Serving: Calories: 486;Fat: 29g;Protein: 4.2g;Carbs: 63g.

Spicy Tofu Tacos With Cherry Tomato Salsa

Servings: 4
Cooking Time: 11 Minutes

Ingredients:
- Cherry Tomato Salsa:
- ¼ cup sliced cherry tomatoes
- ½ jalapeño, deseeded and sliced
- Juice of 1 lime
- 1 garlic clove, minced
- Sea salt and freshly ground black pepper, to taste
- 2 teaspoons extra-virgin olive oil
- Spicy Tofu Taco Filling:
- 4 tablespoons water, divided
- ½ cup canned black beans, rinsed and drained
- 2 teaspoons fresh chopped chives, divided
- ¾ teaspoon ground cumin, divided
- ¾ teaspoon smoked paprika, divided
- Dash cayenne pepper (optional)
- ¼ teaspoon sea salt
- ¼ teaspoon freshly ground black pepper
- 1 teaspoon extra-virgin olive oil
- 6 ounces firm tofu, drained, rinsed, and pressed
- 4 corn tortillas
- ¼ avocado, sliced
- ¼ cup fresh cilantro

Directions:
1. Make the Cherry Tomato Salsa:
2. Combine the ingredients for the salsa in a small bowl. Stir to mix well. Set aside until ready to use.
3. Make the Spicy Tofu Taco Filling:
4. Add 2 tablespoons of water into a saucepan, then add the black beans and sprinkle with 1 teaspoon of chives, ½ teaspoon of cumin, ¼ teaspoon of smoked paprika, and cayenne. Stir to mix well.
5. Cook for 5 minutes over medium heat until heated through, then mash the black beans with the back of a spoon. Turn off the heat and set aside.
6. Add remaining water into a bowl, then add the remaining chives, cumin, and paprika. Sprinkle with cayenne, salt, and black pepper. Stir to mix well. Set aside.
7. Heat the olive oil in a nonstick skillet over medium heat until shimmering.
8. Add the tofu and drizzle with taco sauce, then sauté for 5 minutes or until the seasoning is absorbed. Remove the tofu from the skillet and set aside.
9. Warm the tortillas in the skillet for 1 minutes or until heated through.
10. Transfer the tortillas onto a large plate and top with tofu, mashed black beans, avocado, cilantro, then drizzle the tomato salsa over. Serve immediately.

Nutrition Info:
- Info Per Serving: Calories: 240;Fat: 9.0g;Protein: 11.6g;Carbs: 31.6g.

Chia & Almond Oatmeal

Servings: 2
Cooking Time: 10 Min + Chilling Time

Ingredients:
- ¼ tsp almond extract
- ½ cup milk
- ½ cup rolled oats
- 2 tbsp almonds, sliced
- 2 tbsp sugar
- 1 tsp chia seeds
- ¼ tsp ground cardamom
- ¼ tsp ground cinnamon

Directions:
1. Combine the milk, oats, almonds, sugar, chia seeds, cardamom, almond extract, and cinnamon in a mason jar and shake well. Keep in the refrigerator for 4 hours. Serve.

Nutrition Info:
- Info Per Serving: Calories: 131;Fat: 6.2g;Protein: 4.9g;Carbs: 17g.

Mushroom And Caramelized Onion Musakhan

Servings: 4
Cooking Time: 1 Hour 5 Minutes

Ingredients:
- 2 tablespoons sumac, plus more for sprinkling
- 1 teaspoon ground allspice
- ½ teaspoon ground cardamom
- ½ teaspoon ground cumin
- 3 tablespoons extra-virgin olive oil, divided
- 2 pounds portobello mushroom caps, gills removed, caps halved and sliced ½ inch thick
- 3 medium white onions, coarsely chopped
- ¼ cup water
- Kosher salt, to taste
- 1 whole-wheat Turkish flatbread
- ¼ cup pine nuts
- 1 lemon, wedged

Directions:
1. Preheat the oven to 350ºF.
2. Combine 2 tablespoons of sumac, allspice, cardamom, and cumin in a small bowl. Stir to mix well.
3. Heat 2 tablespoons of olive oil in an oven-proof skillet over medium-high heat until shimmering.
4. Add the mushroom to the skillet and sprinkle with half of sumac mixture. Sauté for 8 minutes or until the mushrooms are tender. You may need to work in batches to avoid overcrowding. Transfer the mushrooms to a plate and set side.
5. Heat 1 tablespoon of olive oil in the skillet over medium-high heat until shimmering.
6. Add the onion and sauté for 20 minutes or until caramelized. Sprinkle with remaining sumac mixture, then cook for 1 more minute.
7. Pour in the water and sprinkle with salt. Bring to a simmer.
8. Turn off the heat and put the mushroom back to the skillet.
9. Place the skillet in the preheated oven and bake for 30 minutes.
10. Remove the skillet from the oven and let the mushroom sit for 10 minutes until cooled down.
11. Heat the Turkish flatbread in a baking dish in the oven for 5 minutes or until warmed through.
12. Arrange the bread on a large plate and top with mushrooms, onions, and roasted pine nuts. Squeeze the lemon wedges over and sprinkle with more sumac. Serve immediately.

Nutrition Info:
- Info Per Serving: Calories: 336;Fat: 18.7g;Protein: 11.5g;Carbs: 34.3g.

Chocolate-strawberry Smoothie

Servings: 2
Cooking Time: 5 Minutes
Ingredients:
- 1 cup buttermilk
- 2 cups strawberries, hulled
- 1 cup crushed ice
- 3 tbsp cocoa powder
- 3 tbsp honey
- 2 mint leaves

Directions:
1. In a food processor, pulse buttermilk, strawberries, ice, cocoa powder, mint, and honey until smooth. Serve.

Nutrition Info:
- Info Per Serving: Calories: 209;Fat: 2.6g;Protein: 7g;Carbs: 47.2g.

Roasted Vegetable Panini

Servings: 4
Cooking Time: 15 Minutes
Ingredients:
- 2 tablespoons extra-virgin olive oil, divided
- 1½ cups diced broccoli
- 1 cup diced zucchini
- ¼ cup diced onion
- ¼ teaspoon dried oregano
- ⅛ teaspoon kosher or sea salt
- ⅛ teaspoon freshly ground black pepper
- 1 jar roasted red peppers, drained and finely chopped
- 2 tablespoons grated Parmesan or Asiago cheese
- 1 cup fresh Mozzarella, sliced
- 1 whole-grain Italian loaf, cut into 4 equal lengths
- Cooking spray

Directions:
1. Place a large, rimmed baking sheet in the oven. Preheat the oven to 450ºF with the baking sheet inside.
2. In a large bowl, stir together 1 tablespoon of the oil, broccoli, zucchini, onion, oregano, salt and pepper.
3. Remove the baking sheet from the oven and spritz the baking sheet with cooking spray. Spread the vegetable mixture on the baking sheet and roast for 5 minutes, stirring once halfway through cooking.
4. Remove the baking sheet from the oven. Stir in the red peppers and Parmesan cheese.
5. In a large skillet over medium-high heat, heat the remaining 1 tablespoon of the oil.
6. Cut open each section of bread horizontally, but don't cut all the way through. Fill each with the vegetable mix (about ½ cup), and layer 1 ounce of sliced Mozzarella cheese on top. Close the sandwiches, and place two of them on the skillet. Place a heavy object on top and grill for 2½ minutes. Flip the sandwiches and grill for another 2½ minutes.
7. Repeat the grilling process with the remaining two sandwiches.
8. Serve hot.

Nutrition Info:
- Info Per Serving: Calories: 116;Fat: 4.0g;Protein: 12.0g;Carbs: 9.0g.

Banana & Chocolate Porridge

Servings: 4
Cooking Time: 20 Minutes

Ingredients:

- 2 bananas
- 4 dried apricots, chopped
- 1 cup barley, soaked
- 2 tbsp flax seeds
- 1 tbsp cocoa powder
- 1 cup coconut milk
- ¼ tsp mint leaves
- 2 oz dark chocolate bars, grated
- 2 tbsp coconut flakes

Directions:

1. Place the barley in a saucepan along with the flaxseeds and two cups of water. Bring to a boil, then lower the heat and simmer for 12 minutes, stirring often.
2. Meanwhile, in a food processor, blend bananas, cocoa powder, coconut milk, apricots, and mint leaves until smooth. Once the barley is ready, stir in chocolate. Add in banana mixture. Garnish with coconut flakes. Serve.

Nutrition Info:

- Info Per Serving: Calories: 476;Fat: 22g;Protein: 10g;Carbs: 65g.

Pumpkin-yogurt Parfaits

Servings: 4
Cooking Time: 5 Min + Chilling Time

Ingredients:

- 1 can pumpkin puree
- 4 tsp honey
- 1 tsp pumpkin pie spice
- ¼ tsp ground cinnamon
- 2 cups Greek yogurt
- 1 cup honey granola
- 2 tbsp pomegranate seeds

Directions:

1. Mix the pumpkin puree, honey, pumpkin pie spice, and cinnamon in a large bowl. Layer the pumpkin mix, yogurt, and granola in small glasses. Repeat the layers. Top with pomegranate seeds. Chill for at least 3 hours before serving.

Nutrition Info:

- Info Per Serving: Calories: 264;Fat: 9.2g;Protein: 15g;Carbs: 35g.

Quick & Easy Bread In A Mug

Servings: 1
Cooking Time: 10 Minutes

Ingredients:

- 1 tbsp olive oil
- 3 tbsp flour
- 1 large egg
- ½ tsp dried thyme
- ¼ tsp baking powder
- ½ tsp salt

Directions:

1. In a heat-resistant ramekin, mix the flour, olive oil, egg, thyme, baking powder, and salt with a fork. Place in the microwave and heat for 80 seconds on high. Run a knife around the edges and flip around to remove the bread. Slice in half to use it to make sandwiches.

Nutrition Info:

- Info Per Serving: Calories: 232;Fat: 22.2g;Protein: 8g;Carbs: 1.1g.

Mango-yogurt Smoothie

Servings: 2
Cooking Time: 5 Minutes
Ingredients:
- 6 oz Greek yogurt
- 2 mangoes, chopped
- 2 tbsp milk
- 7-8 ice cubes

Directions:
1. In a food processor, place the mango, milk, yogurt, and ice cubes. Pulse until creamy and smooth. Serve right away.

Nutrition Info:
- Info Per Serving: Calories: 261;Fat: 2g;Protein: 12g;Carbs: 54g.

White Pizzas With Arugula And Spinach

Servings: 4
Cooking Time: 20 Minutes
Ingredients:
- 1 pound refrigerated fresh pizza dough
- 2 tablespoons extra-virgin olive oil, divided
- ½ cup thinly sliced onion
- 2 garlic cloves, minced
- 3 cups baby spinach
- 3 cups arugula
- 1 tablespoon water
- ¼ teaspoon freshly ground black pepper
- 1 tablespoon freshly squeezed lemon juice
- ½ cup shredded Parmesan cheese
- ½ cup crumbled goat cheese
- Cooking spray

Directions:
1. Preheat the oven to 500°F. Spritz a large, rimmed baking sheet with cooking spray.
2. Take the pizza dough out of the refrigerator.
3. Heat 1 tablespoon of the oil in a large skillet over medium heat. Add the onion to the skillet and cook for 4 minutes, stirring constantly. Add the garlic and cook for 1 minute, stirring constantly.
4. Stir in the spinach, arugula, water and pepper. Cook for about 2 minutes, stirring constantly, or until all the greens are coated with oil and they start to cook down. Remove the skillet from the heat and drizzle with the lemon juice.
5. On a lightly floured work surface, form the pizza dough into a 12-inch circle or a 10-by-12-inch rectangle, using a rolling pin or by stretching with your hands.
6. Place the dough on the prepared baking sheet. Brush the dough with the remaining 1 tablespoon of the oil. Spread the cooked greens on top of the dough to within ½ inch of the edge. Top with the Parmesan cheese and goat cheese.
7. Bake in the preheated oven for 10 to 12 minutes, or until the crust starts to brown around the edges.
8. Remove from the oven and transfer the pizza to a cutting board. Cut into eight pieces before serving.

Nutrition Info:
- Info Per Serving: Calories: 521;Fat: 31.0g;Protein: 23.0g;Carbs: 38.0g.

Maple Berry & Walnut Oatmeal

Servings:2
Cooking Time:10 Minutes
Ingredients:
- 1 cup mixed berries
- 1 ½ cups rolled oats
- 2 tbsp walnuts, chopped
- 2 tsp maple syrup

Directions:
1. Cook the oats according to the package instructions and share in 2 bowls. Microwave the maple syrup and berries for 30 seconds; stir well. Pour over each bowl. Top with walnuts.

Nutrition Info:
- Info Per Serving: Calories: 262;Fat: 10g;Protein: 15g;Carbs: 57g.

Honey & Feta Frozen Yogurt

Servings:4
Cooking Time:5 Minutes + Freezing Time
Ingredients:
- 1 tbsp honey
- 1 cup Greek yogurt
- ½ cup feta cheese, crumbled
- 2 tbsp mint leaves, chopped

Directions:
1. In a food processor, blend yogurt, honey, and feta cheese until smooth. Transfer to a wide dish, cover with plastic wrap, and put in the freezer for 2 hours or until solid. When frozen, spoon into cups, sprinkle with mint, and serve.

Nutrition Info:
- Info Per Serving: Calories: 170;Fat: 12g;Protein: 7g;Carbs: 13g.

Kale And Apple Smoothie

Servings:2
Cooking Time: 0 Minutes
Ingredients:
- 2 cups shredded kale
- 1 cup unsweetened almond milk
- ¼ cup 2 percent plain Greek yogurt
- ½ Granny Smith apple, unpeeled, cored and chopped
- ½ avocado, diced
- 3 ice cubes

Directions:
1. Put all ingredients in a blender and blend until smooth and thick.
2. Pour into two glasses and serve immediately.

Nutrition Info:
- Info Per Serving: Calories: 177;Fat: 6.8g;Protein: 8.2g;Carbs: 22.0g.

Cherry Tomato & Mushroom Frittata

Servings: 4
Cooking Time: 30 Minutes

Ingredients:
- 1 cup Italian brown mushrooms, sliced
- 2 tbsp olive oil
- 2 spring onions, chopped
- 8 cherry tomatoes, halved
- 6 eggs
- ½ cup milk
- Salt and black pepper to taste
- ¼ cup grated Parmesan
- ½ tbsp Italian seasoning mix

Directions:
1. Preheat oven to 370 F. Mix eggs, milk, Italian seasoning, salt, and pepper in a bowl. Warm olive oil in a skillet over medium heat until sizzling. Add in mushrooms, spring onions, and tomatoes and sauté for 5 minutes.
2. Pour in the egg mixture and cook for 5 minutes until the eggs are set. Scatter Parmesan cheese and bake in the oven for 6-7 minutes until the cheese melts. Slice before serving.

Nutrition Info:
- Info Per Serving: Calories: 227;Fat: 15g;Protein: 13g;Carbs: 13g.

Savory Breakfast Oatmeal

Servings: 2
Cooking Time: 15 Minutes

Ingredients:
- ½ cup steel-cut oats
- 1 cup water
- 1 medium cucumber, chopped
- 1 large tomato, chopped
- 1 tablespoon olive oil
- Pinch freshly grated Parmesan cheese
- Sea salt and freshly ground pepper, to taste
- Flat-leaf parsley or mint, chopped, for garnish

Directions:
1. Combine the oats and water in a medium saucepan and bring to a boil over high heat, stirring continuously, or until the water is absorbed, about 15 minutes.
2. Divide the oatmeal between 2 bowls and scatter the tomato and cucumber on top. Drizzle with the olive oil and sprinkle with the Parmesan cheese.
3. Season with salt and pepper to taste. Serve garnished with the parsley.

Nutrition Info:
- Info Per Serving: Calories: 197;Fat: 8.9g;Protein: 6.3g;Carbs: 23.1g.

Crustless Tiropita (greek Cheese Pie)

Servings: 6
Cooking Time: 35 To 40 Minutes

Ingredients:
- 4 tablespoons extra-virgin olive oil, divided
- ½ cup whole-milk ricotta cheese
- 1¼ cups crumbled feta cheese
- 1 tablespoon chopped fresh dill
- 2 tablespoons chopped fresh mint
- ½ teaspoon lemon zest
- ¼ teaspoon freshly ground black pepper
- 2 large eggs
- ½ teaspoon baking powder

Directions:
1. Preheat the oven to 350ºF. Coat the bottom and sides of a baking dish with 2 tablespoons of olive oil. Set aside.
2. Mix together the ricotta and feta cheese in a medium bowl and stir with a fork until well combined. Add the dill, mint, lemon zest, and black pepper and mix well.
3. In a separate bowl, whisk together the eggs and baking powder. Pour the whisked eggs into the bowl of cheese mixture. Blend well.
4. Slowly pour the mixture into the coated baking dish and drizzle with the remaining 2 tablespoons of olive oil.
5. Bake in the preheated oven for about 35 to 40 minutes, or until the pie is browned around the edges and cooked through.
6. Cool for 5 minutes before slicing into wedges.

Nutrition Info:
- Info Per Serving: Calories: 181;Fat: 16.6g;Protein: 7.0g;Carbs: 1.8g.

Egg Bake

Servings: 2
Cooking Time: 30 Minutes

Ingredients:
- 1 tablespoon olive oil
- 1 slice whole-grain bread
- 4 large eggs
- 3 tablespoons unsweetened almond milk
- ½ teaspoon onion powder
- ¼ teaspoon garlic powder
- ¾ cup chopped cherry tomatoes
- ¼ teaspoon salt
- Pinch freshly ground black pepper

Directions:
1. Preheat the oven to 375ºF.
2. Coat two ramekins with the olive oil and transfer to a baking sheet. Line the bottom of each ramekin with ½ of bread slice.
3. In a medium bowl, whisk together the eggs, almond milk, onion powder, garlic powder, tomatoes, salt, and pepper until well combined.
4. Pour the mixture evenly into two ramekins. Bake in the preheated oven for 30 minutes, or until the eggs are completely set.
5. Cool for 5 minutes before serving.

Nutrition Info:
- Info Per Serving: Calories: 240;Fat: 17.4g;Protein: 9.0g;Carbs: 12.2g.

Energy Nut Smoothie

Servings: 1
Cooking Time: 10 Minutes

Ingredients:
- 1 tbsp extra-virgin olive oil
- ½ cup Greek yogurt
- ½ cup almond milk
- ½ orange, zested and juiced
- 1 tbsp pistachios, chopped
- 1 tsp honey
- ½ tsp ground allspice
- ¼ tsp ground cinnamon
- ¼ tsp vanilla extract

Directions:
1. Place the yogurt, almond milk, orange zest and juice, olive oil, pistachios, honey, allspice, cinnamon, and vanilla in a blender and pulse until smooth and creamy. Add a little water to achieve your desired consistency. Serve in a chilled glass.

Nutrition Info:
- Info Per Serving: Calories: 264;Fat: 22.2g;Protein: 6g;Carbs: 12g.

Basil Scrambled Eggs

Servings: 2
Cooking Time: 8 Minutes

Ingredients:
- 4 large eggs
- 2 tablespoons grated Gruyère cheese
- 2 tablespoons finely chopped fresh basil
- 1 tablespoon plain Greek yogurt
- 1 tablespoon olive oil
- 2 cloves garlic, minced
- Sea salt and freshly ground pepper, to taste

Directions:
1. In a large bowl, beat together the eggs, cheese, basil, and yogurt with a whisk until just combined.
2. Heat the oil in a large, heavy nonstick skillet over medium-low heat. Add the garlic and cook until golden, about 1 minute.
3. Pour the egg mixture into the skillet over the garlic. Work the eggs continuously and cook until fluffy and soft.
4. Season with sea salt and freshly ground pepper to taste. Divide between 2 plates and serve immediately.

Nutrition Info:
- Info Per Serving: Calories: 243;Fat: 19.7g;Protein: 15.6g;Carbs: 3.4g.

Easy Alfalfa Sprout And Nut Rolls

Servings: 16
Cooking Time: 0 Minutes
Ingredients:
- 1 cup alfalfa sprouts
- 2 tablespoons Brazil nuts
- ½ cup chopped fresh cilantro
- 2 tablespoons flaked coconut
- 1 garlic clove, minced
- 2 tablespoons ground flaxseeds
- Zest and juice of 1 lemon
- Pinch cayenne pepper
- Sea salt and freshly ground black pepper, to taste
- 1 tablespoon melted coconut oil
- 2 tablespoons water
- 2 whole-grain wraps

Directions:
1. Combine all ingredients, except for the wraps, in a food processor, then pulse to combine well until smooth.
2. Unfold the wraps on a clean work surface, then spread the mixture over the wraps. Roll the wraps up and refrigerate for 30 minutes until set.
3. Remove the rolls from the refrigerator and slice into 16 bite-sized pieces, if desired, and serve.

Nutrition Info:
- Info Per Serving: Calories: 67;Fat: 7.1g;Protein: 2.2g;Carbs: 2.9g.

Tomato And Egg Scramble

Servings: 4
Cooking Time: 20 Minutes
Ingredients:
- 2 tablespoons extra-virgin olive oil
- ¼ cup finely minced red onion
- 1½ cups chopped fresh tomatoes
- 2 garlic cloves, minced
- ½ teaspoon dried thyme
- ½ teaspoon dried oregano
- 8 large eggs
- ½ teaspoon salt
- ¼ teaspoon freshly ground black pepper
- ¾ cup crumbled feta cheese
- ¼ cup chopped fresh mint leaves

Directions:
1. Heat the olive oil in a large skillet over medium heat.
2. Sauté the red onion and tomatoes in the hot skillet for 10 to 12 minutes, or until the tomatoes are softened.
3. Stir in the garlic, thyme, and oregano and sauté for 2 to 4 minutes, or until the garlic is fragrant.
4. Meanwhile, beat the eggs with the salt and pepper in a medium bowl until frothy.
5. Pour the beaten eggs into the skillet and reduce the heat to low. Scramble
6. for 3 to 4 minutes, stirring constantly, or until the eggs are set.
7. Remove from the heat and scatter with the feta cheese and mint. Serve warm.

Nutrition Info:
- Info Per Serving: Calories: 260;Fat: 21.9g;Protein: 10.2g;Carbs: 5.8g.

Beans , Grains, And Pastas Recipes

Slow Cooker Pork & Bean Cassoulet

Servings:4
Cooking Time:hours 10 Minutes
Ingredients:
- ½ cup apricots, cut into quarters
- 2 lb pork stew meat, cubed
- ½ cup vegetable stock
- 1 tbsp ginger, grated
- 1 tsp coriander, ground
- 2 tsp cumin, ground
- Salt and black pepper to taste
- 14 oz canned tomatoes, diced
- 1 red onion, chopped
- 2 garlic cloves, minced
- 15 oz canned cannellini beans
- 1 tbsp cilantro, chopped

Directions:
1. Place pork, vegetable stock, ginger, coriander, cumin, salt, pepper, tomatoes, onion, garlic, and apricots in your slow cooker. Put the lid and cook for 6 hours on Low. Open the lid and add in beans and cook for another 2 hours on Low. Adjust the seasoning, top with cilantro, and serve.

Nutrition Info:
- Info Per Serving: Calories: 290;Fat: 13g;Protein: 26g;Carbs: 30g.

Veggie & Egg Quinoa With Pancetta

Servings:4
Cooking Time:35 Minutes
Ingredients:
- 4 pancetta slices, cooked and crumbled
- 2 tbsp olive oil
- 1 small red onion, chopped
- 1 red bell pepper, chopped
- 1 sweet potato, grated
- 1 green bell pepper, chopped
- 2 garlic cloves, minced
- 1 cup mushrooms, sliced
- ½ cup quinoa
- 1 cup chicken stock
- 4 eggs, fried
- ¼ tsp red pepper flakes
- Salt and black pepper to taste

Directions:
1. Warm the olive oil in a skillet over medium heat and cook onion, garlic, bell peppers, sweet potato, and mushrooms for 5 minutes, stirring often. Stir in quinoa for another minute. Mix in stock, salt, and pepper for 15 minutes. Share into plates and serve topped with fried eggs, salt, pepper, red pepper flakes, and crumbled pancetta.

Nutrition Info:
- Info Per Serving: Calories: 310;Fat: 15g;Protein: 16g;Carbs: 26g.

Swiss Chard Couscous With Feta Cheese

Servings: 4
Cooking Time: 20 Minutes
Ingredients:
- 2 tbsp olive oil
- 10 oz couscous
- 2 garlic cloves, minced
- 1 cup raisins
- ½ cup feta cheese, crumbled
- 1 bunch of Swiss chard, torn

Directions:
1. In a bowl, place couscous and cover with hot water. Let sit covered for 10 minutes. Using a fork, fluff it. Warm the olive oil in a skillet over medium heat and sauté garlic for a minute. Stir in couscous, raisins, and chard. Top with feta.

Nutrition Info:
- Info Per Serving: Calories: 310;Fat: 8g;Protein: 7g;Carbs: 18g.

Smoky Paprika Chickpeas

Servings: 4
Cooking Time: 30 Minutes
Ingredients:
- ¼ cup extra-virgin olive oil
- 4 garlic cloves, sliced thin
- ½ tsp red pepper flakes
- 1 onion, chopped fine
- Salt and black pepper to taste
- 1 tsp smoked paprika
- 2 cans chickpeas
- 1 cup chicken broth
- 2 tbsp minced fresh parsley
- 2 tsp lemon juice

Directions:
1. Warm 3 tbsp of olive oil in a skillet over medium heat. Cook garlic and pepper flakes until the garlic turns golden but not brown, about 3 minutes. Stir in onion and salt and cook until softened and lightly browned, 5 minutes. Stir in smoked paprika, chickpeas, and broth and bring to a boil. Simmer covered for 7 minutes until chickpeas are heated through.
2. Uncover, increase the heat to high, and continue to cook until nearly all liquid has evaporated, about 3 minutes. Remove and stir in parsley and lemon juice. Season with salt and pepper and drizzle with remaining olive oil. Serve warm.

Nutrition Info:
- Info Per Serving: Calories: 223;Fat: 11.4g;Protein: 7g;Carbs: 25g.

Lemony Tuna Barley With Capers

Servings: 4
Cooking Time: 50 Minutes
Ingredients:
- 2 tbsp olive oil
- 3 cups chicken stock
- 10 oz canned tuna, flaked
- 1 cup barley
- Salt and black pepper to taste
- 12 cherry tomatoes, halved
- ½ cup pepperoncini, sliced
- ¼ cup capers, drained
- ½ lemon, juiced

Directions:
1. Boil chicken stock in a saucepan over medium heat and add in barley. Cook covered for 40 minutes. Fluff the barley and remove to a bowl. Stir in tuna, salt, pepper, tomatoes, pepperoncini, olive oil, capers, and lemon juice. Serve.

Nutrition Info:
- Info Per Serving: Calories: 260;Fat: 12g;Protein: 24g;Carbs: 17g.

Rosemary Barley With Walnuts

Servings:4
Cooking Time:45 Minutes
Ingredients:
- 2 tbsp olive oil
- ½ cup diced onion
- ½ cup diced celery
- 1 carrot, peeled and diced
- 3 cups water
- 1 cup barley
- ½ tsp thyme
- ½ tsp rosemary
- ¼ cup pine nuts
- Salt and black pepper to taste

Directions:
1. Warm the olive oil in a medium saucepan over medium heat. Sauté the onion, celery, and carrot over medium heat until tender. Add the water, barley, and seasonings, and bring to a boil. Reduce the heat and simmer for 23 minutes or until tender. Stir in the pine nuts and season to taste. Serve warm.

Nutrition Info:
- Info Per Serving: Calories: 276;Fat: 9g;Protein: 7g;Carbs: 41g.

Black Bean & Chickpea Burgers

Servings:4
Cooking Time:35 Minutes
Ingredients:
- 1 tsp olive oil
- 1 can black beans
- 1 can chickpeas
- ½ white onion, chopped
- 2 garlic cloves, minced
- 2 free-range eggs
- 1 tsp ground cumin
- Salt and black pepper to taste
- 1 cup panko breadcrumbs
- ½ cup old-fashioned rolled oats
- 6 hamburger buns, halved
- 2 avocados
- 2 tbsp lemon juice
- 6 large lettuce leaves

Directions:
1. Preheat oven to 380 F. Blitz the black beans, chickpeas, eggs, cumin, salt, and pepper in a food processor until smooth. Transfer the mixture to a bowl and add the onion and garlic and mix well. Stir in the bread crumbs and oats. Shape the mixture into 6 balls, flatten them with your hands to make patties. Brush both sides of the burgers with oil. Arrange them on a parchment-lined baking sheet. Bake for 30 minutes, flippingonce until slightly crispy on the edges.
2. Meanwhile, mash the avocado with the lemon juice and a pinch of salt with a fork until smooth; set aside. Toast the buns for 2-3 minutes. Spread the avocado mixture onto the base of each bun, then top with the burgers and lettuce leaves. Finish with the bun tops. Serve and enjoy!

Nutrition Info:
- Info Per Serving: Calories: 867;Fat: 22g;Protein: 39g;Carbs: 133g.

Two-bean Cassoulet

Servings:4
Cooking Time:40 Minutes
Ingredients:
- 2 tbsp olive oil
- 1 cup canned pinto beans
- 1 cup canned can kidney beans
- 2 red bell peppers, chopped
- 1 onion, chopped
- 1 celery stalk, chopped
- 2 garlic cloves, minced
- 1 can diced tomatoes
- 1 tbsp red pepper flakes
- 1 tsp ground cumin
- Salt and black pepper to taste
- ¼ tsp ground coriander

Directions:
1. Warm olive oil in a pot over medium heat and sauté bell peppers, celery, garlic, and onion for 5 minutes until tender. Stir in ground cumin, ground coriander, salt, and pepper for 1 minute. Pour in beans, tomatoes, and red pepper flakes. Bring to a boil, then decrease the heat and simmer for another 20 minutes. Serve immediately.

Nutrition Info:
- Info Per Serving: Calories: 361;Fat: 8.4g;Protein: 17g;Carbs: 56g.

Fofu Spaghetti Bolognese

Servings:4
Cooking Time:25 Minutes
Ingredients:
- 2 tbsp olive oil
- 16 oz spaghetti, broken in half
- 1 cup crumbled firm tofu
- 1 medium onion, chopped
- 2 celery stalks, chopped
- 1 garlic clove, minced
- 1 bay leaf
- 2 cups passata
- ¼ cup vegetable broth
- Salt and black pepper to taste
- 1 small bunch basil, chopped
- 1 cup grated Parmesan cheese

Directions:
1. In a pot of boiling water, cook the spaghetti pasta for 8-10 minutes until al dente. Drain and set aside.
2. Heat the olive oil in a large pot and cook the tofu until brown, 5 minutes. Stir in the onion, celery, and cook until softened, 5 minutes. Add garlic, bay leaf and cook until fragrant, 30 seconds. Mix in passata, broth and season with salt and pepper. Cook until the sauce thickens, 8-10 minutes. Open the lid, stir in the basil and adjust the taste with salt and pepper. Divide the spaghetti between plates and top with the sauce. Sprinkle the Parmesan cheese and serve.

Nutrition Info:
- Info Per Serving: Calories: 424;Fat: 19g;Protein: 22g;Carbs: 31g.

Autumn Vegetable & Rigatoni Bake

Servings: 6
Cooking Time: 45 Minutes

Ingredients:
- 2 tbsp grated Pecorino-Romano cheese
- 2 tbsp olive oil
- 1 lb pumpkin, chopped
- 1 zucchini, chopped
- 1 onion, chopped
- 1 lb rigatoni
- Salt and black pepper to taste
- ½ tsp garlic powder
- ½ cup dry white wine

Directions:
1. Preheat oven to 420 F. Combine zucchini, pumpkin, onion, and olive oil in a bowl. Arrange on a lined aluminum foil sheet and season with salt, pepper, and garlic powder. Bake for 30 minutes until tender. In a pot of boiling water, cook rigatoni for 8-10 minutes until al dente. Drain and set aside.
2. In a food processor, place ½ cup of the roasted veggies and wine and pulse until smooth. Transfer to a skillet over medium heat. Stir in rigatoni and cook until heated through. Top with the remaining vegetables and Pecorino cheese to serve.

Nutrition Info:
- Info Per Serving: Calories: 186; Fat: 11g; Protein: 10g; Carbs: 15g.

Turkish-style Orzo

Servings: 2
Cooking Time: 10 Minutes

Ingredients:
- 1 cup dry orzo
- 1 cup halved grape tomatoes
- 1 bag baby spinach
- 2 tbsp extra-virgin olive oil
- Salt and black pepper to taste
- ¾ cup feta cheese, crumbled
- 1 lemon, juiced and zested
- 1 tbsp fresh dill, chopped

Directions:
1. In a pot of boiling water, cook the orzo for 8 minutes. Drain well and return to the pot. Add in the tomatoes and spinach and cook until the spinach is wilted, 4-5 minutes. Mix in the olive oil, salt, and pepper. Top the dish with feta, dill, lemon juice, and lemon zest, then toss to coat. Serve and enjoy!

Nutrition Info:
- Info Per Serving: Calories: 612; Fat: 27g; Protein: 22g; Carbs: 74g.

Mushroom & Green Onion Rice Pilaf

Servings: 4
Cooking Time: 30 Minutes

Ingredients:
- 2 tbsp olive oil
- 1 cup rice, rinsed
- 2 greens onions, chopped
- 2 cups chicken stock
- 1 cup mushrooms, sliced
- 1 garlic clove, minced
- Salt and black pepper to taste
- ½ cup Parmesan cheese, grated
- 2 tbsp cilantro, chopped

Directions:
1. Warm the olive oil in a skillet over medium heat and cook onion, garlic, and mushrooms for 5 minutes until tender. Stir in rice, salt, and pepper for 1 minute. Pour in chicken stock and cook for 15-18 minutes. Transfer to a platter, scatter Parmesan cheese all over, and sprinkle with cilantro to serve.

Nutrition Info:
- Info Per Serving: Calories: 250; Fat: 10g; Protein: 13g; Carbs: 28g.

Slow Cooked Turkey And Brown Rice

Servings: 6
Cooking Time: 3 Hours 10 Minutes

Ingredients:

- 1 tablespoon extra-virgin olive oil
- 1½ pounds ground turkey
- 2 tablespoons chopped fresh sage, divided
- 2 tablespoons chopped fresh thyme, divided
- 1 teaspoon sea salt
- ½ teaspoon ground black pepper
- 2 cups brown rice
- 1 can stewed tomatoes, with the juice
- ¼ cup pitted and sliced Kalamata olives
- 3 medium zucchini, sliced thinly
- ¼ cup chopped fresh flat-leaf parsley
- 1 medium yellow onion, chopped
- 1 tablespoon plus 1 teaspoon balsamic vinegar
- 2 cups low-sodium chicken stock
- 2 garlic cloves, minced
- ½ cup grated Parmesan cheese, for serving

Directions:

1. Heat the olive oil in a nonstick skillet over medium-high heat until shimmering.
2. Add the ground turkey and sprinkle with 1 tablespoon of sage, 1 tablespoon of thyme, salt and ground black pepper.
3. Sauté for 10 minutes or until the ground turkey is lightly browned.
4. Pour them in the slow cooker, then pour in the remaining ingredients, except for the Parmesan. Stir to mix well.
5. Put the lid on and cook on high for 3 hours or until the rice and vegetables are tender.
6. Pour them in a large serving bowl, then spread with Parmesan cheese before serving.

Nutrition Info:

- Info Per Serving: Calories: 499;Fat: 16.4g;Protein: 32.4g;Carbs: 56.5g.

Vegetable Quinoa & Garbanzo Skillet

Servings: 4
Cooking Time: 30 Minutes

Ingredients:

- 2 tbsp olive oil
- 1 shallot, chopped
- 2 garlic cloves, minced
- 1 tomato, chopped
- 1 cup quinoa
- 1 eggplant, cubed
- ¼ cup green olives, chopped
- ½ cup feta cheese, crumbled
- 1 cup canned garbanzo beans
- Salt and black pepper to taste

Directions:

1. Warm the olive oil in a skillet over medium heat and sauté garlic, shallot, tomato, and eggplant for 4-5 minutes until tender. Pour in quinoa and 2 cups of water. Season with salt and pepper and bring to a boil. Reduce the heat to low and cook for 15 minutes. Stir in olives, feta, and garbanzo beans.

Nutrition Info:

- Info Per Serving: Calories: 320;Fat: 12g;Protein: 12g;Carbs: 45g.

Creamy Asparagus & Parmesan Linguine

Servings: 2
Cooking Time: 30 Minutes

Ingredients:
- 2 tsp olive oil
- 1 bunch of asparagus spears
- 1 yellow onion, thinly sliced
- ¼ cup white wine
- ¼ cup vegetable stock
- 2 cups heavy cream
- ¼ tsp garlic powder
- 8 oz linguine
- ¼ cup Parmesan cheese
- 1 lemon, juiced
- Salt and black pepper to taste
- 2 tbsp chives, chopped

Directions:
1. Bring to a boil salted water in a pot over high heat. Add the linguine and cook according to package directions. Drain and transfer to a bowl. Slice the asparagus into bite-sized pieces. Warm the olive oil in a skillet over medium heat. Add onion and cook 3 minutes until softened. Add asparagus and wine and cook until wine is mostly evaporated, then add the stock. Stir in cream and garlic powder and bring to a boil and simmer until the sauce is slightly thick, 2-3 minutes. Add the linguine and stir until everything is heated through. Remove from the heat and season with lemon juice, salt, and pepper. Top with parmesan cheese and chives and serve.

Nutrition Info:
- Info Per Serving: Calories: 503; Fat: 55g; Protein: 24g; Carbs: 41g.

Simple Green Rice

Servings: 4
Cooking Time: 35 Minutes

Ingredients:
- 2 tbsp butter
- 4 spring onions, sliced
- 1 leek, sliced
- 1 medium zucchini, chopped
- 5 oz broccoli florets
- 2 oz curly kale
- ½ cup frozen green peas
- 2 cloves garlic, minced
- 1 thyme sprig, chopped
- 1 rosemary sprig, chopped
- 1 cup white rice
- 2 cups vegetable broth
- 1 large tomato, chopped
- 2 oz Kalamata olives, sliced

Directions:
1. Melt the butter in a saucepan over medium heat. Cook the spring onions, leek, and zucchini for about 4-5 minutes or until tender. Add in the garlic, thyme, and rosemary and continue to sauté for about 1 minute or until aromatic. Add in the rice, broth, and tomato. Bring to a boil, turn the heat to a gentle simmer, and cook for about 10-12 minutes. Stir in broccoli, kale, and green peas, and continue cooking for 5 minutes. Fluff the rice with a fork and garnish with olives.

Nutrition Info:
- Info Per Serving: Calories: 403; Fat: 11g; Protein: 9g; Carbs: 64g.

Cherry, Apricot, And Pecan Brown Rice Bowl

Servings: 2
Cooking Time: 1 Hour 1 Minutes

Ingredients:
- 2 tablespoons olive oil
- 2 green onions, sliced
- ½ cup brown rice
- 1 cup low-sodium chicken stock
- 2 tablespoons dried cherries
- 4 dried apricots, chopped
- 2 tablespoons pecans, toasted and chopped
- Sea salt and freshly ground pepper, to taste

Directions:
1. Heat the olive oil in a medium saucepan over medium-high heat until shimmering.
2. Add the green onions and sauté for 1 minutes or until fragrant.
3. Add the rice. Stir to mix well, then pour in the chicken stock.
4. Bring to a boil. Reduce the heat to low. Cover and simmer for 50 minutes or until the brown rice is soft.
5. Add the cherries, apricots, and pecans, and simmer for 10 more minutes or until the fruits are tender.
6. Pour them in a large serving bowl. Fluff with a fork. Sprinkle with sea salt and freshly ground pepper. Serve immediately.

Nutrition Info:
- Info Per Serving: Calories: 451;Fat: 25.9g;Protein: 8.2g;Carbs: 50.4g.

Paprika Spinach & Chickpea Bowl

Servings: 4
Cooking Time: 20 Minutes

Ingredients:
- 2 tbsp olive oil
- 1 lb canned chickpeas
- 10 oz spinach
- 1 tsp coriander seeds
- 1 red onion, finely chopped
- 2 tomatoes, pureed
- 1 garlic clove, minced
- ½ tbsp rosemary
- ½ tsp smoked paprika
- Salt and white pepper to taste

Directions:
1. Heat the olive oil in a pot over medium heat. Add in the onion, garlic, coriander seeds, salt, and pepper and cook for 3 minutes until translucent. Stir in tomatoes, rosemary, paprika, salt, and white pepper. Bring to a boil, then lower the heat, and simmer for 10 minutes. Add in chickpeas and spinach and cook covered until the spinach wilts. Serve.

Nutrition Info:
- Info Per Serving: Calories: 512;Fat: 1.8g;Protein: 25g;Carbs: 76g.

Asparagus & Goat Cheese Rice Salad

Servings:4
Cooking Time:35 Minutes
Ingredients:
- 3 tbsp olive oil
- ½ cups brown rice
- Salt and black pepper to taste
- ½ lemon, zested and juiced
- 1 lb asparagus, chopped
- 1 shallot, minced
- 2 oz goat cheese, crumbled
- ¼ cup hazelnuts, toasted
- ¼ cup parsley, minced

Directions:
1. In a pot, bring 2 cups of water to a boil. Add rice, a pinch of salt, and cook until tender, 15-18 minutes, stirring occasionally. Drain the rice, spread onto a rimmed baking sheet, and drizzle with 1 tbsp of lemon juice. Let cool completely, 15 minutes.
2. Heat 1 tbsp of olive oil in a skillet over high heat. Add asparagus, salt, and pepper to taste and cook until asparagus is browned and crisp-tender, 4-5 minutes. Transfer to plate and let cool slightly. Whisk the remaining oil, lemon zest and juice, shallot in large a bowl. Add rice, asparagus, half of the goat cheese, half of the hazelnuts, and half of the parsley. Toss to combine and let sit for 10 minutes. Season with salt and pepper to taste. Sprinkle with the remaining goat cheese, hazelnuts, and parsley.

Nutrition Info:
- Info Per Serving: Calories: 185;Fat: 16g;Protein: 8g;Carbs: 24g.

Swoodles With Almond Butter Sauce

Servings:4
Cooking Time: 20 Minutes
Ingredients:
- Sauce:
- 1 garlic clove
- 1-inch piece fresh ginger, peeled and sliced
- ¼ cup chopped yellow onion
- ¾ cup almond butter
- 1 tablespoon tamari
- 1 tablespoon raw honey
- 1 teaspoon paprika
- 1 tablespoon fresh lemon juice
- ⅛ teaspoon ground red pepper
- Sea salt and ground black pepper, to taste
- ¼ cup water
- Swoodles:
- 2 large sweet potatoes, spiralized
- 2 tablespoons coconut oil, melted
- Sea salt and ground black pepper, to taste
- For Serving:
- ½ cup fresh parsley, chopped
- ½ cup thinly sliced scallions

Directions:
1. Make the Sauce
2. Put the garlic, ginger, and onion in a food processor, then pulse to combine well.
3. Add the almond butter, tamari, honey, paprika, lemon juice, ground red pepper, salt, and black pepper to the food processor. Pulse to combine well. Pour in the water during the pulsing until the mixture is thick and smooth.
4. Make the Swoodles:
5. Preheat the oven to 425°F. Line a baking sheet with parchment paper.
6. Put the spiralized sweet potato in a bowl, then drizzle with olive oil. Toss to coat well. Transfer them on the baking sheet. Sprinkle with salt and pepper.
7. Bake in the preheated oven for 20 minutes or until lightly browned and al dente. Check the doneness during the baking and remove any well-cooked swoodles.
8. Transfer the swoodles on a large plate and spread with sauce, parsley, and scallions. Toss to serve.

Nutrition Info:
- Info Per Serving: Calories: 441;Fat: 33.6g;Protein: 12.0g;Carbs: 29.6g.

Chili Pork Rice

Servings: 4
Cooking Time: 8 Hours 10 Minutes
Ingredients:
- 3 tbsp olive oil
- 2 lb pork loin, sliced
- 1 cup chicken stock
- ½ tbsp chili powder
- 2 tsp thyme, dried
- ½ tbsp garlic powder
- Salt and black pepper to taste
- 2 cups rice, cooked

Directions:
1. Place pork, chicken stock, oil, chili powder, garlic powder, salt, and pepper in your slow cooker. Cover with the lid and cook for 8 hours on Low. Share pork into plates with a side of rice and garnish with thyme to serve.

Nutrition Info:
- Info Per Serving: Calories: 280;Fat: 15g;Protein: 15g;Carbs: 17g.

Creamy Shrimp With Tie Pasta

Servings: 4
Cooking Time: 25 Minutes
Ingredients:
- 1 lb shrimp, peeled and deveined
- 1 tbsp olive oil
- 2 tbsp unsalted butter
- Salt and black pepper to taste
- 6 garlic cloves, minced
- ½ cup dry white wine
- 1 ½ cups heavy cream
- ½ cup grated Asiago cheese
- 2 tbsp chopped fresh parsley
- 16 oz bow tie pasta
- Salt to taste

Directions:
1. In a pot of boiling salted water, cook the tie pasta for 8-10 minutes until al dente. Drain and set aside.
2. Heat the olive oil in a large skillet, season the shrimp with salt and black pepper, and cook in the oil on both sides until pink and opaque, 2 minutes. Set aside. Melt the butter in the skillet and sauté the garlic until fragrant. Stir in the white wine and cook until reduced by half, scraping the bottom of the pan to deglaze. Reduce the heat to low and stir in the heavy cream. Allow simmering for 1 minute and stir in the Asiago cheese to melt. Return the shrimp to the sauce and sprinkle the parsley on top. Adjust the taste with salt and black pepper, if needed. Top the pasta with sauce and serve.

Nutrition Info:
- Info Per Serving: Calories: 493;Fat: 32g;Protein: 34g;Carbs: 16g.

Lemon-basil Spaghetti

Servings:6
Cooking Time:30 Minutes
Ingredients:
- ½ cup extra-virgin olive oil
- Zest and juice from 1 lemon
- 1 garlic clove, minced
- Salt and black pepper to taste
- 2 oz ricotta cheese, chopped
- 1 lb spaghetti
- 6 tbsp shredded fresh basil

Directions:
1. In a bowl, whisk oil, grated lemon zest, juice, garlic, salt, and pepper. Stir in ricotta cheese and mix well. Meanwhile, bring a pot filled with salted water to a boil. Cook the pasta until al dente. Reserve ½ cup of the cooking liquid, then drain pasta and return it to the pot. Add oil mixture and basil and toss to combine. Season to taste and adjust consistency with reserved cooking water as needed. Serve warm.

Nutrition Info:
- Info Per Serving: Calories: 395;Fat: 11g;Protein: 10g;Carbs: 37g.

Carrot & Caper Chickpeas

Servings:4
Cooking Time:35 Minutes
Ingredients:
- 3 tbsp olive oil
- 3 tbsp capers, drained
- 1 lemon, juiced and zested
- 1 red onion, chopped
- 14 oz canned chickpeas
- 4 carrots, peeled and cubed
- 1 tbsp parsley, chopped
- Salt and black pepper to taste

Directions:
1. Warm the olive oil in a skillet over medium heat and cook onion, lemon zest, lemon juice, and capers for 5 minutes. Stir in chickpeas, carrots, parsley, salt, and pepper and cook for another 20 minutes. Serve and enjoy!

Nutrition Info:
- Info Per Serving: Calories: 210;Fat: 5g;Protein: 4g;Carbs: 7g.

Hearty Butternut Spinach, And Cheeses Lasagna

Servings: 4
Cooking Time: 3 Hours 45 Minutes

Ingredients:

- 2 tablespoons extra-virgin olive oil, divided
- 1 butternut squash, halved lengthwise and deseeded
- ½ teaspoon sage
- ½ teaspoon sea salt
- ¼ teaspoon ground black pepper
- ¼ cup grated Parmesan cheese
- 2 cups ricotta cheese
- ½ cup unsweetened almond milk
- 5 layers whole-wheat lasagna noodles
- 4 ounces fresh spinach leaves, divided
- ½ cup shredded part skim Mozzarella, for garnish

Directions:

1. Preheat the oven to 400ºF. Line a baking sheet with parchment paper.
2. Brush 1 tablespoon of olive oil on the cut side of the butternut squash, then place the squash on the baking sheet.
3. Bake in the preheated oven for 45 minutes or until the squash is tender.
4. Allow to cool until you can handle it, then scoop the flesh out and put the flesh in a food processor to purée.
5. Combine the puréed butternut squash flesh with sage, salt, and ground black pepper in a large bowl. Stir to mix well.
6. Combine the cheeses and milk in a separate bowl, then sprinkle with salt and pepper, to taste.
7. Grease the slow cooker with 1 tablespoon of olive oil, then add a layer of lasagna noodles to coat the bottom of the slow cooker.
8. Spread half of the squash mixture on top of the noodles, then top the squash mixture with another layer of lasagna noodles.
9. Spread half of the spinach over the noodles, then top the spinach with half of cheese mixture. Repeat with remaining 3 layers of lasagna noodles, squash mixture, spinach, and cheese mixture.
10. Top the cheese mixture with Mozzarella, then put the lid on and cook on low for 3 hours or until the lasagna noodles are al dente.
11. Serve immediately.

Nutrition Info:

- Info Per Serving: Calories: 657;Fat: 37.1g;Protein: 30.9g;Carbs: 57.2g.

Bean And Veggie Pasta

Servings: 2
Cooking Time: 15 Minutes

Ingredients:

- 16 ounces small whole wheat pasta, such as penne, farfalle, or macaroni
- 5 cups water
- 1 can cannellini beans, drained and rinsed
- 1 can diced (with juice) or crushed tomatoes
- 1 yellow onion, chopped
- 1 red or yellow bell pepper, chopped
- 2 tablespoons tomato paste
- 1 tablespoon olive oil
- 3 garlic cloves, minced
- ¼ teaspoon crushed red pepper (optional)
- 1 bunch kale, stemmed and chopped
- 1 cup sliced basil
- ½ cup pitted Kalamata olives, chopped

Directions:

1. Add the pasta, water, beans, tomatoes (with juice if using diced), onion, bell pepper, tomato paste, oil, garlic, and crushed red pepper (if desired), to a large stockpot or deep skillet with a lid. Bring to a boil over high heat, stirring often.
2. Reduce the heat to medium-high, add the kale, and cook, continuing to stir often, until the pasta is al dente, about 10 minutes.
3. Remove from the heat and let sit for 5 minutes. Garnish with the basil and olives and serve.

Nutrition Info:

- Info Per Serving: Calories: 565;Fat: 17.7g;Protein: 18.0g;Carbs: 85.5g.

Fish And Seafood Recipes

Avocado Shrimp Ceviche

Servings:4
Cooking Time: 0 Minutes
Ingredients:
- 1 pound fresh shrimp, peeled, deveined, and cut in half lengthwise
- 1 small red or yellow bell pepper, cut into ½-inch chunks
- ½ small red onion, cut into thin slivers
- ½ English cucumber, peeled and cut into ½-inch chunks
- ¼ cup chopped fresh cilantro
- ½ cup extra-virgin olive oil
- ⅓ cup freshly squeezed lime juice
- 2 tablespoons freshly squeezed clementine juice
- 2 tablespoons freshly squeezed lemon juice
- 1 teaspoon salt
- ½ teaspoon freshly ground black pepper
- 2 ripe avocados, peeled, pitted, and cut into ½-inch chunks

Directions:
1. Place the shrimp, bell pepper, red onion, cucumber, and cilantro in a large bowl and toss to combine.
2. In a separate bowl, stir together the olive oil, lime, clementine, and lemon juice, salt, and black pepper until smooth. Pour the mixture into the bowl of shrimp and vegetable mixture and toss until they are completely coated.
3. Cover the bowl with plastic wrap and transfer to the refrigerator to marinate for at least 2 hours, or up to 8 hours.
4. When ready, stir in the avocado chunks and toss to incorporate. Serve immediately.

Nutrition Info:
- Info Per Serving: Calories: 496;Fat: 39.5g;Protein: 25.3g;Carbs: 13.8g.

Crab Stuffed Celery Sticks

Servings:4
Cooking Time:10 Minutes
Ingredients:
- 1 cup cream cheese
- 6 oz crab meat
- 1 tsp Mediterranean seasoning
- 2 tbsp apple cider vinegar
- 8 celery sticks, halved
- Salt and black pepper to taste

Directions:
1. In a mixing bowl, combine the cream cheese, crab meat, apple cider vinegar, salt, pepper, and Mediterranean seasoning. Divide the crab mixture between the celery sticks. Serve.

Nutrition Info:
- Info Per Serving: Calories: 30;Fat: 2g;Protein: 3g;Carbs: 1g.

Baked Salmon With Tarragon Mustard Sauce

Servings:4
Cooking Time: 12 Minutes
Ingredients:

- 1¼ pounds salmon fillet (skin on or removed), cut into 4 equal pieces
- ¼ cup Dijon mustard
- ¼ cup avocado oil mayonnaise
- Zest and juice of ½ lemon
- 2 tablespoons chopped fresh tarragon
- ½ teaspoon salt
- ¼ teaspoon freshly ground black pepper
- 4 tablespoons extra-virgin olive oil, for serving

Directions:
1. Preheat the oven to 425ºF. Line a baking sheet with parchment paper.
2. Arrange the salmon pieces on the prepared baking sheet, skin-side down.
3. Stir together the mustard, avocado oil mayonnaise, lemon zest and juice, tarragon, salt, and pepper in a small bowl. Spoon the mustard mixture over the salmon.
4. Bake for 10 to 12 minutes, or until the top is golden and salmon is opaque in the center.
5. Divide the salmon among four plates and drizzle each top with 1 tablespoon of olive oil before serving.

Nutrition Info:
- Info Per Serving: Calories: 386;Fat: 27.7g;Protein: 29.3g;Carbs: 3.8g.

Cod Fillets In Mushroom Sauce

Servings:4
Cooking Time:45 Minutes
Ingredients:

- 2 cups cremini mushrooms, sliced
- ¼ cup olive oil
- 4 cod fillets
- ½ cup shallots, chopped
- 2 garlic cloves, minced
- 2 cups canned diced tomatoes
- ½ cup clam juice
- ¼ tsp chili flakes
- ¼ tsp sweet paprika
- 1 tbsp capers
- ¼ cup raisins, soaked
- 1 lemon, cut into wedges
- Salt to taste

Directions:
1. Heat the oil in a skillet over medium heat. Sauté shallots and garlic for 2-3 minutes. Add in mushrooms and cook for another 4 minutes. Stir in tomatoes, clam juice, chili flakes, paprika, capers, and salt. Bring to a boil and simmer for 15 minutes.
2. Preheat oven to 380 F. Arrange the cod fillets on a greased baking pan. Cover with the mushroom mixture and top with the soaked raisins. Bake for 18-20 minutes. Serve garnished with lemon wedges.

Nutrition Info:
- Info Per Serving: Calories: 317;Fat: 13g;Protein: 25g;Carbs: 26g.

Leek & Olive Cod Casserole

Servings:4
Cooking Time:30 Minutes
Ingredients:
- ½ cup olive oil
- 1 lb fresh cod fillets
- 1 cup black olives, chopped
- 4 leeks, trimmed and sliced
- 1 cup breadcrumbs
- ¾ cup chicken stock
- Salt and black pepper to taste

Directions:
1. Preheat oven to 350 F. Brush the cod with some olive oil, season with salt and pepper, and bake for 5-7 minutes. Let it cool, then cut it into 1-inch pieces.
2. Warm the remaining olive oil in a skillet over medium heat. Stir-fry the olives and leeks for 4 minutes until the leeks are tender. Add the breadcrumbs and chicken stock, stirring to mix. Fold in the pieces of cod. Pour the mixture into a greased baking dish and bake for 15 minutes or until cooked through.

Nutrition Info:
- Info Per Serving: Calories: 534;Fat: 33g;Protein: 24g;Carbs: 36g.

Baked Halibut Steaks With Vegetables

Servings:4
Cooking Time: 20 Minutes
Ingredients:
- 2 teaspoon olive oil, divided
- 1 clove garlic, peeled and minced
- ½ cup minced onion
- 1 cup diced zucchini
- 2 cups diced fresh tomatoes
- 2 tablespoons chopped fresh basil
- ¼ teaspoon salt
- ¼ teaspoon ground black pepper
- 4 halibut steaks
- ⅓ cup crumbled feta cheese

Directions:
1. Preheat oven to 450°F. Coat a shallow baking dish lightly with 1 teaspoon of olive oil.
2. In a medium saucepan, heat the remaining 1 teaspoon of olive oil.
3. Add the garlic, onion, and zucchini and mix well. Cook for 5 minutes, stirring occasionally, or until the zucchini is softened.
4. Remove the saucepan from the heat and stir in the tomatoes, basil, salt, and pepper.
5. Place the halibut steaks in the coated baking dish in a single layer. Spread the zucchini mixture evenly over the steaks. Scatter the top with feta cheese.
6. Bake in the preheated oven for about 15 minutes, or until the fish flakes when pressed lightly with a fork. Serve hot.

Nutrition Info:
- Info Per Serving: Calories: 258;Fat: 7.6g;Protein: 38.6g;Carbs: 6.5g.

Grilled Lemon Pesto Salmon

Servings: 2
Cooking Time: 6 To 10 Minutes
Ingredients:
- 10 ounces salmon fillet
- Salt and freshly ground black pepper, to taste
- 2 tablespoons prepared pesto sauce
- 1 large fresh lemon, sliced
- Cooking spray

Directions:
1. Preheat the grill to medium-high heat. Spray the grill grates with cooking spray.
2. Season the salmon with salt and black pepper. Spread the pesto sauce on top.
3. Make a bed of fresh lemon slices about the same size as the salmon fillet on the hot grill, and place the salmon on top of the lemon slices. Put any additional lemon slices on top of the salmon.
4. Grill the salmon for 6 to 10 minutes, or until the fish is opaque and flakes apart easily.
5. Serve hot.

Nutrition Info:
- Info Per Serving: Calories: 316;Fat: 21.1g;Protein: 29.0g;Carbs: 1.0g.

Caper & Herring Stuffed Eggs

Servings: 6
Cooking Time: 20 Minutes
Ingredients:
- 1/3 cup aioli
- 1 tbsp capers, drained
- 12 eggs
- 1 tbsp tarragon, chopped
- 2 pickled jalapenos, minced
- Salt and black pepper to taste
- 1 can smoked herring
- 1 tsp paprika

Directions:
1. Fill a pot over medium heat with water by 1 inch. Bring to a boil. Carefully add the eggs, one at a time to the pot, cover, and boil them for 10 minutes. Cool the eggs in cold water.
2. Peel the eggs and slice them in half lengthwise; mix the yolks with the aioli, herring, paprika, capers, tarragon, jalapenos, salt, and pepper. Divide the mixture between the egg whites. Arrange the deviled eggs on a serving platter.

Nutrition Info:
- Info Per Serving: Calories: 205;Fat: 13g;Protein: 18g;Carbs: 4g.

Calamari In Garlic-cilantro Sauce

Servings: 4
Cooking Time: 25 Minutes
Ingredients:
- 2 tbsp olive oil
- 2 lb calamari, sliced into rings
- 4 garlic cloves, minced
- 1 lime, juiced
- 2 tbsp balsamic vinegar
- 3 tbsp cilantro, chopped

Directions:
1. Warm the olive oil in a skillet over medium heat and sauté garlic, lime juice, balsamic vinegar, and cilantro for 5 minutes. Stir in calamari rings and cook for 10 minutes.

Nutrition Info:
- Info Per Serving: Calories: 290;Fat: 19g;Protein: 19g;Carbs: 10g.

Seafood Stew

Servings: 4
Cooking Time: 25 Minutes

Ingredients:
- ½ lb skinless trout, cubed
- 2 tbsp olive oil
- ½ lb clams
- ½ lb cod, cubed
- 1 onion, chopped
- ½ fennel bulb, chopped
- 2 garlic cloves, minced
- ¼ cup dry white wine
- 2 tbsp chopped fresh parsley
- 1 can tomato sauce
- 1 cup fish broth
- 1 tbsp Italian seasoning
- ⅛ tsp red pepper flakes
- Salt and black pepper to taste

Directions:
1. Warm olive oil in a pot over medium heat and sauté onion and fennel for 5 minutes. Add in garlic and cook for 30 seconds. Pour in the wine and cook for 1 minute. Stir in tomato sauce, clams, broth, cod, trout, salt, Italian seasoning, red pepper flakes, and pepper. Bring just a boil and simmer for 5 minutes. Discard any unopened clams. Top with parsley.

Nutrition Info:
- Info Per Serving: Calories: 372;Fat: 15g;Protein: 34g;Carbs: 25g.

Seared Halibut With Moroccan Chermoula

Servings: 4
Cooking Time: 30 Min + Marinating Time

Ingredients:
- 2 tbsp olive oil
- 1 tsp dry thyme
- 1 tsp dry rosemary
- 4 halibut steaks
- Salt and black pepper to taste
- Chermoula
- 2 tbsp olive oil
- ¾ cup fresh cilantro
- 2 tbsp lemon juice
- 4 garlic cloves, minced
- ½ tsp ground cumin
- ½ tsp paprika
- ¼ tsp salt
- ½ tsp cayenne pepper

Directions:
1. In a large bowl, coat the fish with 2 tbsp olive oil, rosemary, thyme, salt, and pepper. Let it marinate for 15 minutes. Process cilantro, lemon juice, olive oil, garlic, cumin, paprika, salt, and cayenne pepper in your food processor until smooth, about 1 minute, scraping down sides of the bowl as needed. Set aside the chermoula until ready to serve.
2. Preheat oven to 325 F. Place the halibut in a baking tray. Bake for 10-12 minutes until halibut flakes apart when gently prodded with a paring knife. Serve with chermoula.

Nutrition Info:
- Info Per Serving: Calories: 187;Fat: 11g;Protein: 19g;Carbs: 1.1g.

Lemony Sea Bass

Servings: 4
Cooking Time: 25 Minutes
Ingredients:
- 1 tbsp butter, melted
- 4 skinless sea bass fillets
- Salt and black pepper to taste
- ½ tsp onion powder

Directions:
1. Preheat oven to 425 F. Rub the fish with salt, pepper, and onion powder and place on a greased baking dish. Drizzle the butter all over and bake for 20 minutes or until opaque.

Nutrition Info:
- Info Per Serving: Calories: 159;Fat: 6g;Protein: 23.8g;Carbs: 1.2g.

Spicy Grilled Shrimp With Lemon Wedges

Servings: 6
Cooking Time: 6 Minutes
Ingredients:
- 1 large clove garlic, crushed
- 1 teaspoon coarse salt
- 1 teaspoon paprika
- ½ teaspoon cayenne pepper
- 2 teaspoons lemon juice
- 2 tablespoons plus 1 teaspoon olive oil, divided
- 2 pounds large shrimp, peeled and deveined
- 8 wedges lemon, for garnish

Directions:
1. Preheat the grill to medium heat.
2. Stir together the garlic, salt, paprika, cayenne pepper, lemon juice, and 2 tablespoons of olive oil in a small bowl until a paste forms. Add the shrimp and toss until well coated.
3. Grease the grill grates lightly with remaining 1 teaspoon of olive oil.
4. Grill the shrimp for 4 to 6 minutes, flipping the shrimp halfway through, or until the shrimp is totally pink and opaque.
5. Garnish the shrimp with lemon wedges and serve hot.

Nutrition Info:
- Info Per Serving: Calories: 163;Fat: 5.8g;Protein: 25.2g;Carbs: 2.8g.

Dill Chutney Salmon

Servings: 2
Cooking Time: 3 Minutes

Ingredients:

- Chutney:
- ¼ cup fresh dill
- ¼ cup extra virgin olive oil
- Juice from ½ lemon
- Sea salt, to taste
- Fish:
- 2 cups water
- 2 salmon fillets
- Juice from ½ lemon
- ¼ teaspoon paprika
- Salt and freshly ground pepper to taste

Directions:

1. Pulse all the chutney ingredients in a food processor until creamy. Set aside.
2. Add the water and steamer basket to the Instant Pot. Place salmon fillets, skin-side down, on the steamer basket. Drizzle the lemon juice over salmon and sprinkle with the paprika.
3. Secure the lid. Select the Manual mode and set the cooking time for 3 minutes at High Pressure.
4. Once cooking is complete, do a quick pressure release. Carefully open the lid.
5. Season the fillets with pepper and salt to taste. Serve topped with the dill chutney.

Nutrition Info:

- Info Per Serving: Calories: 636;Fat: 41.1g;Protein: 65.3g;Carbs: 1.9g.

Cheesy Smoked Salmon Crostini

Servings: 4
Cooking Time: 10 Min + Chilling Time

Ingredients:

- 4 oz smoked salmon, sliced
- 2 oz feta cheese, crumbled
- 4 oz cream cheese, softened
- 2 tbsp horseradish sauce
- 2 tsp orange zest
- 1 red onion, chopped
- 2 tbsp chives, chopped
- 1 baguette, sliced and toasted

Directions:

1. In a bowl, mix cream cheese, horseradish sauce, onion, feta cheese, and orange zest until smooth. Spread the mixture on the baguette slices. Top with salmon and chives to serve.

Nutrition Info:

- Info Per Serving: Calories: 290;Fat: 19g;Protein: 26g;Carbs: 5g.

Roasted Cod With Cabbage

Servings: 4
Cooking Time: 30 Minutes

Ingredients:

- 2 tbsp olive oil
- 1 head white cabbage, shredded
- 1 tsp garlic powder
- 1 tsp smoked paprika
- 4 cod fillets, boneless
- ½ cup tomato sauce
- 1 tsp Italian seasoning
- 1 tbsp chives, chopped

Directions:

1. Preheat the oven to 390F. Mix cabbage, garlic powder, paprika, olive oil, tomato sauce, Italian seasoning, and chives in a roasting pan. Top with cod fillets and bake covered with foil for 20 minutes. Serve immediately.

Nutrition Info:

- Info Per Serving: Calories: 200;Fat: 14g;Protein: 18g;Carbs: 24g.

Baked Cod With Vegetables

Servings: 2
Cooking Time: 25 Minutes
Ingredients:

- 1 pound thick cod fillet, cut into 4 even portions
- ¼ teaspoon onion powder (optional)
- ¼ teaspoon paprika
- 3 tablespoons extra-virgin olive oil
- 4 medium scallions
- ½ cup fresh chopped basil, divided
- 3 tablespoons minced garlic (optional)
- 2 teaspoons salt
- 2 teaspoons freshly ground black pepper
- ¼ teaspoon dry marjoram (optional)
- 6 sun-dried tomato slices
- ½ cup dry white wine
- ½ cup crumbled feta cheese
- 1 can oil-packed artichoke hearts, drained
- 1 lemon, sliced
- 1 cup pitted kalamata olives
- 1 teaspoon capers (optional)
- 4 small red potatoes, quartered

Directions:
1. Preheat the oven to 375°F.
2. Season the fish with paprika and onion powder (if desired).
3. Heat an ovenproof skillet over medium heat and sear the top side of the cod for about 1 minute until golden. Set aside.
4. Heat the olive oil in the same skillet over medium heat. Add the scallions, ¼ cup of basil, garlic (if desired), salt, pepper, marjoram (if desired), tomato slices, and white wine and stir to combine. Bring to a boil and remove from heat.
5. Evenly spread the sauce on the bottom of skillet. Place the cod on top of the tomato basil sauce and scatter with feta cheese. Place the artichokes in the skillet and top with the lemon slices.
6. Scatter with the olives, capers (if desired), and the remaining ¼ cup of basil. Remove from the heat and transfer to the preheated oven. Bake for 15 to 20 minutes, or until it flakes easily with a fork.
7. Meanwhile, place the quartered potatoes on a baking sheet or wrapped in aluminum foil. Bake in the oven for 15 minutes until fork-tender.
8. Cool for 5 minutes before serving.

Nutrition Info:
- Info Per Serving: Calories: 1168;Fat: 60.0g;Protein: 63.8g;Carbs: 94.0g.

One-skillet Salmon With Olives & Escarole

Servings: 4
Cooking Time: 25 Minutes
Ingredients:

- 3 tbsp olive oil
- 1 head escarole, torn
- 4 salmon fillets, boneless
- 1 lime, juiced
- Salt and black pepper to taste
- ¼ cup fish stock
- ¼ cup green olives, pitted and chopped
- ¼ cup fresh chives, chopped

Directions:

1. Warm half of the olive oil in a skillet over medium heat and sauté escarole, lime juice, salt, pepper, fish stock, and olives for 6 minutes. Share into plates. Warm the remaining oil in the same skillet. Sprinkle salmon with salt and pepper and fry for 8 minutes on both sides until golden brown. Transfer to the escarole plates and serve warm topped with chives.

Nutrition Info:
- Info Per Serving: Calories: 280;Fat: 15g;Protein: 19g;Carbs: 25g.

Herby Cod Skewers

Servings: 4
Cooking Time: 30 Minutes
Ingredients:
- 1 lb cod fillets, cut into chunks
- 2 sweet peppers, cut into chunks
- 2 tbsp olive oil
- 2 oranges, juiced
- 1 tbsp Dijon mustard
- 1 tsp dried dill
- 1 tsp dried parsley
- Salt and black pepper to taste

Directions:
1. Mix olive oil, orange juice, dill, parsley, mustard, salt, and pepper in a bowl. Stir in cod to coat. Allow sitting for 10 minutes. Heat the grill over medium heat. Thread the cod and peppers onto skewers. Grill for 7-8 minutes, turning regularly until the fish is cooked through.

Nutrition Info:
- Info Per Serving: Calories: 244;Fat: 8g;Protein: 27g;Carbs: 15.5g.

Pan-seared Trout With Tzatziki

Servings: 4
Cooking Time: 20 Minutes
Ingredients:
- 1 cucumber, grated and squeezed
- 3 tbsp olive oil
- 4 trout fillets, boneless
- ½ lime, juiced
- Salt and black pepper to taste
- 1 garlic clove, minced
- 1 tsp sweet paprika
- 4 garlic cloves, minced
- 2 cups Greek yogurt
- 1 tbsp dill, chopped

Directions:
1. Warm 2 tbsp of the olive oil in a skillet over medium heat. Sprinkle the trout with salt, pepper, lime juice, garlic, and paprika and sear for 8 minutes on all sides. Remove to a paper towel–lined plate. Combine cucumber, garlic, remaining olive oil, yogurt, salt, and dill in a bowl. Share trout into plates and serve with tzatziki.

Nutrition Info:
- Info Per Serving: Calories: 400;Fat: 19g;Protein: 41g;Carbs: 19g.

Drunken Mussels With Lemon-butter Sauce

Servings: 4
Cooking Time: 15 Minutes
Ingredients:
- 4 lb mussels, cleaned
- 4 tbsp butter
- ½ cup chopped parsley
- 1 white onion, chopped
- 2 cups dry white wine
- ½ tsp sea salt
- 6 garlic cloves, minced
- Juice of ½ lemon

Directions:
1. Add wine, garlic, salt, onion, and ¼ cup of parsley in a pot over medium heat and let simmer. Put in mussels and simmer covered for 7-8 minutes. Divide mussels between four bowls. Stir butter and lemon juice into the pot and drizzle over the mussels. Top with parsley and serve.

Nutrition Info:
- Info Per Serving: Calories: 487;Fat: 18g;Protein: 37g;Carbs: 26g.

Parchment Orange & Dill Salmon

Servings: 4
Cooking Time: 25 Minutes

Ingredients:

- 2 tbsp butter, melted
- 4 salmon fillets
- Salt and black pepper to taste
- 1 orange, juiced and zested
- 4 tbsp fresh dill, chopped

Directions:

1. Preheat oven to 375 F. Coat the salmon fillets on both sides with butter. Season with salt and pepper and divide them between 4 pieces of parchment paper. Drizzle the orange juice over each piece of fish and top with orange zest and dill. Wrap the paper around the fish to make packets. Place on a baking sheet and bake for 15-20 minutes until the cod is cooked through. Serve and enjoy!

Nutrition Info:

- Info Per Serving: Calories: 481;Fat: 21g;Protein: 65g;Carbs: 4.2g.

Sole Piccata With Capers

Servings: 4
Cooking Time: 17 Minutes

Ingredients:

- 1 teaspoon extra-virgin olive oil
- 4 sole fillets, patted dry
- 3 tablespoons almond butter
- 2 teaspoons minced garlic
- 2 tablespoons all-purpose flour
- 2 cups low-sodium chicken broth
- Juice and zest of ½ lemon
- 2 tablespoons capers

Directions:

1. Place a large skillet over medium-high heat and add the olive oil.
2. Sear the sole fillets until the fish flakes easily when tested with a fork, about 4 minutes on each side. Transfer the fish to a plate and set aside.
3. Return the skillet to the stove and add the butter.
4. Sauté the garlic until translucent, about 3 minutes.
5. Whisk in the flour to make a thick paste and cook, stirring constantly, until the mixture is golden brown, about 2 minutes.
6. Whisk in the chicken broth, lemon juice and zest.
7. Cook for about 4 minutes until the sauce is thickened.
8. Stir in the capers and serve the sauce over the fish.

Nutrition Info:

- Info Per Serving: Calories: 271;Fat: 13.0g;Protein: 30.0g;Carbs: 7.0g.

Rosemary Wine Poached Haddock

Servings: 4
Cooking Time: 40 Minutes

Ingredients:

- 4 haddock fillets
- Salt and black pepper to taste
- 2 garlic cloves, minced
- ½ cup dry white wine
- ½ cup seafood stock
- 4 rosemary sprigs for garnish

Directions:

1. Preheat oven to 380 F. Sprinkle haddock fillets with salt and black pepper and arrange them on a baking dish. Pour in the wine, garlic, and stock. Bake covered for 20 minutes until the fish is tender; remove to a serving plate. Pour the cooking liquid into a pot over high heat. Cook for 10 minutes until reduced by half. Place on serving dishes and top with the reduced poaching liquid. Serve garnished with rosemary.

Nutrition Info:

- Info Per Serving: Calories: 215;Fat: 4g;Protein: 35g;Carbs: 3g.

Garlic Shrimp With Arugula Pesto

Servings: 2
Cooking Time: 5 Minutes

Ingredients:
- 3 cups lightly packed arugula
- ½ cup lightly packed basil leaves
- ¼ cup walnuts
- 3 tablespoons olive oil
- 3 medium garlic cloves
- 2 tablespoons grated Parmesan cheese
- 1 tablespoon freshly squeezed lemon juice
- Salt and freshly ground black pepper, to taste
- 1 package zucchini noodles
- 8 ounces cooked, shelled shrimp
- 2 Roma tomatoes, diced

Directions:
1. Process the arugula, basil, walnuts, olive oil, garlic, Parmesan cheese, and lemon juice in a food processor until smooth, scraping down the sides as needed. Season with salt and pepper to taste.
2. Heat a skillet over medium heat. Add the pesto, zucchini noodles, and cooked shrimp. Toss to combine the sauce over the noodles and shrimp, and cook until heated through.
3. Taste and season with more salt and pepper as needed. Serve topped with the diced tomatoes.

Nutrition Info:
- Info Per Serving: Calories: 435;Fat: 30.2g;Protein: 33.0g;Carbs: 15.1g.

Garlic Shrimp With Mushrooms

Servings: 4
Cooking Time: 15 Minutes

Ingredients:
- 1 pound fresh shrimp, peeled, deveined, and patted dry
- 1 teaspoon salt
- 1 cup extra-virgin olive oil
- 8 large garlic cloves, thinly sliced
- 4 ounces sliced mushrooms (shiitake, baby bella, or button)
- ½ teaspoon red pepper flakes
- ¼ cup chopped fresh flat-leaf Italian parsley

Directions:
1. In a bowl, season the shrimp with salt. Set aside.
2. Heat the olive oil in a large skillet over medium-low heat.
3. Add the garlic and cook for 3 to 4 minutes until fragrant, stirring occasionally.
4. Sauté the mushrooms for 5 minutes, or until they start to exude their juices.
5. Stir in the shrimp and sprinkle with red pepper flakes and sauté for 3 to 4 minutes more, or until the shrimp start to turn pink.
6. Remove the skillet from the heat and add the parsley. Stir to combine and serve warm.

Nutrition Info:
- Info Per Serving: Calories: 619;Fat: 55.5g;Protein: 24.1g;Carbs: 3.7g.

Sides, Salads, And Soups Recipes

Sumptuous Greek Vegetable Salad

Servings: 6
Cooking Time: 0 Minutes
Ingredients:
- Salad:
- 1 can chickpeas, drained and rinsed
- 1 can artichoke hearts, drained and halved
- 1 head Bibb lettuce, chopped
- 1 cucumber, peeled deseeded, and chopped
- 1½ cups grape tomatoes, halved
- ¼ cup chopped basil leaves
- ½ cup sliced black olives
- ½ cup cubed feta cheese
- Dressing:
- 1 tablespoon freshly squeezed lemon juice (from about ½ small lemon)
- ¼ teaspoon freshly ground black pepper
- 1 tablespoon chopped fresh oregano
- 2 tablespoons extra-virgin olive oil
- 1 tablespoon red wine vinegar
- 1 teaspoon honey

Directions:
1. Combine the ingredients for the salad in a large salad bowl, then toss to combine well.
2. Combine the ingredients for the dressing in a small bowl, then stir to mix well.
3. Dressing the salad and serve immediately.

Nutrition Info:
- Info Per Serving: Calories: 165;Fat: 8.1g;Protein: 7.2g;Carbs: 17.9g.

Cucumber & Spelt Salad With Chicken

Servings: 4
Cooking Time: 35 Minutes
Ingredients:
- 4 tbsp olive oil
- ½ lb chicken breasts
- 1 tbsp dill, chopped
- 2 lemons, zested
- Juice of 2 lemons
- 3 tbsp parsley, chopped
- Salt and black pepper to taste
- 1 cup spelt grains
- 1 red leaf lettuce heads, torn
- 1 red onion, sliced
- 10 cherry tomatoes, halved
- 1 cucumber, sliced

Directions:
1. In a bowl, combine dill, lemon zest, lemon juice, 2 tbsp olive oil, parsley, salt, and pepper and mix well. Add in chicken breasts, toss to coat, cover, and refrigerate for 30 minutes. Place spelt grains in a pot and cover with water. Stir in salt and pepper. Put over medium heat and bring to a boil. Cook for 45 minutes and drain. Transfer to a bowl and let it cool.
2. Preheat the grill. Remove the chicken and grill for 12 minutes on all sides. Transfer to a bowl to cool before slicing. Once the spelt is cooled, add in the remaining olive oil, lettuce, onion, tomatoes, and cucumber and toss to coat. Top the salad with sliced chicken and serve.

Nutrition Info:
- Info Per Serving: Calories: 350;Fat: 18g;Protein: 27g;Carbs: 28g.

Ritzy Summer Fruit Salad

Servings: 8
Cooking Time: 0 Minutes

Ingredients:
- Salad:
- 1 cup fresh blueberries
- 2 cups cubed cantaloupe
- 2 cups red seedless grapes
- 1 cup sliced fresh strawberries
- 2 cups cubed honeydew melon
- Zest of 1 large lime
- ½ cup unsweetened toasted coconut flakes
- Dressing:
- ¼ cup raw honey
- Juice of 1 large lime
- ¼ teaspoon sea salt
- ½ cup extra-virgin olive oil

Directions:
1. Combine the ingredients for the salad in a large salad bowl, then toss to combine well.
2. Combine the ingredients for the dressing in a small bowl, then stir to mix well.
3. Dressing the salad and serve immediately.

Nutrition Info:
- Info Per Serving: Calories: 242;Fat: 15.5g;Protein: 1.3g;Carbs: 28.0g.

Chili Lentil Soup

Servings: 4
Cooking Time: 30 Minutes

Ingredients:
- 2 tbsp olive oil
- 1 cup lentils, rinsed
- 1 onion, chopped
- 2 carrots, chopped
- 1 potato, cubed
- 1 tomato, chopped
- 4 garlic cloves, minced
- 4 cups vegetable broth
- ½ tsp chili powder
- Salt and black pepper to taste
- 2 tbsp fresh parsley, chopped

Directions:
1. Warm the olive oil in a pot over medium heat. Add in onion, garlic, and carrots and sauté for 5-6 minutes until tender. Mix in lentils, broth, salt, pepper, chili powder, potato, and tomato. Bring to a boil, lower the heat and simmer for 15-18 minutes, stirring often. Top with parsley and serve.

Nutrition Info:
- Info Per Serving: Calories: 331;Fat: 9g;Protein: 19g;Carbs: 44.3g.

Root Vegetable Roast

Servings: 4
Cooking Time: 25 Minutes
Ingredients:
- 1 bunch beets, peeled and cut into 1-inch cubes
- 2 small sweet potatoes, peeled and cut into 1-inch cubes
- 3 parsnips, peeled and cut into 1-inch rounds
- 4 carrots, peeled and cut into 1-inch rounds
- 1 tablespoon raw honey
- 1 teaspoon sea salt
- ½ teaspoon freshly ground black pepper
- 1 tablespoon extra-virgin olive oil
- 2 tablespoons coconut oil, melted

Directions:
1. Preheat the oven to 400ºF. Line a baking sheet with parchment paper.
2. Combine all the ingredients in a large bowl. Toss to coat the vegetables well.
3. Pour the mixture in the baking sheet, then place the sheet in the preheated oven.
4. Roast for 25 minutes or until the vegetables are lightly browned and soft. Flip the vegetables halfway through the cooking time.
5. Remove the vegetables from the oven and allow to cool before serving.

Nutrition Info:
- Info Per Serving: Calories: 461;Fat: 18.1g;Protein: 5.9g;Carbs: 74.2g.

Arugula & Caper Green Salad

Servings: 4
Cooking Time: 10 Minutes
Ingredients:
- 1 tbsp olive oil
- 10 green olives, sliced
- 4 cups baby arugula
- 1 tbsp capers, drained
- 1 tbsp balsamic vinegar
- 1 tsp lemon zest, grated
- 1 tbsp lemon juice
- 1 tsp parsley, chopped
- Salt and black pepper to taste

Directions:
1. Mix capers, olives, vinegar, lemon zest, lemon juice, oil, parsley, salt, pepper, and arugula in a bowl. Serve.

Nutrition Info:
- Info Per Serving: Calories: 160;Fat: 4g;Protein: 5g;Carbs: 4g.

Collard Green & Rice Salad

Servings: 4
Cooking Time: 10 Minutes
Ingredients:
- 1 tbsp olive oil
- 1 cup white rice
- 10 oz collard greens, torn
- 4 tbsp walnuts, chopped
- 2 tbsp balsamic vinegar
- 4 tbsp tahini paste
- Salt and black pepper to taste
- 2 tbsp parsley, chopped

Directions:
1. Bring to a boil salted water over medium heat. Add in the rice and cook for 15-18 minutes. Drain and rest to cool.
2. Whisk tahini, 4 tbsp of cold water, and vinegar in a bowl. In a separate bowl, combine cooled rice, collard greens, walnuts, salt pepper, olive oil, and tahini dressing. Serve topped with parsley.

Nutrition Info:
- Info Per Serving: Calories: 180;Fat: 4g;Protein: 4g;Carbs: 6g.

Tri-color Salad

Servings:4
Cooking Time:5 Minutes
Ingredients:
- 2 tbsp olive oil
- 1 cucumber, sliced
- 1 lb tomatoes, sliced
- 1 red onion, chopped
- Salt and black pepper to taste
- 4 oz feta cheese, crumbled
- 2 tbsp parsley, chopped

Directions:
1. Combine tomatoes, onion, cucumber, salt, pepper, feta cheese, parsley, and olive oil in a bowl. Serve.

Nutrition Info:
- Info Per Serving: Calories: 200;Fat: 5g;Protein: 4g;Carbs: 9g.

Spinach & Chickpea Soup With Sausages

Servings:4
Cooking Time:35 Minutes
Ingredients:
- 2 tbsp olive oil
- 8 oz Italian sausage, sliced
- 1 can chickpeas
- 4 cups chopped spinach
- 1 onion, chopped
- 1 carrot, chopped
- 1 red bell pepper, chopped
- 3 garlic cloves, minced
- 6 cups chicken broth
- 1 tsp dried oregano
- Salt and black pepper to taste
- ½ tsp red pepper flakes

Directions:
1. Warm olive oil in a pot over medium heat. Sear the sausage for 5 minutes until browned. Set aside.
2. Add carrot, onion, garlic, and bell pepper to the pot and sauté for 5 minutes until soft. Pour in broth, chickpeas, spinach, oregano, salt, pepper, and red flakes; let simmer for 5 minutes until the spinach softens. Bring the sausage back to the pot and cook for another minute. Serve warm.

Nutrition Info:
- Info Per Serving: Calories: 473;Fat: 21g;Protein: 26g;Carbs: 47g.

Zesty Asparagus Salad

Servings:4
Cooking Time:10 Minutes
Ingredients:
- 4 tbsp olive oil
- 1 lb asparagus
- 1 garlic clove, minced
- Salt and black pepper to taste
- 1 tbsp balsamic vinegar
- 1 tbsp lemon zest

Directions:
1. Roast the asparagus in a greased skillet over medium heat for 5-6 minutes, turning once. Season to taste. Toss with garlic, olive oil, lemon zest, and vinegar. Serve.

Nutrition Info:
- Info Per Serving: Calories: 148;Fat: 13.6g;Protein: 3g;Carbs: 5.7g.

Feta & Cannellini Bean Soup

Servings:4
Cooking Time:30 Minutes
Ingredients:
- 2 tbsp olive oil
- 4 oz feta cheese, crumbled
- 1 cup collard greens, torn
- 2 cups canned cannellini beans
- 1 fennel bulb, chopped
- 1 carrot, chopped
- ½ cup spring onions, chopped
- ½ tsp dried rosemary
- ½ tsp dried basil
- 1 garlic clove, minced
- 4 cups vegetable broth
- 2 tbsp tomato paste
- Salt and black pepper to taste

Directions:
1. In a pot over medium heat, warm the olive oil. Add in fennel, garlic, carrot, and spring onions and sauté until tender, about 2-3 minutes. Stir in tomato paste, rosemary, and basil and cook for 2 more minutes. Pour in vegetable broth and cannellini beans. Bring to a boil, then lower the heat, and simmer for 15 minutes. Add in collard greens and cook for another 2-3 minutes until wilted. Adjust the seasoning with salt and pepper. Top with feta cheese and serve.

Nutrition Info:
- Info Per Serving: Calories: 519;Fat: 15g;Protein: 32g;Carbs: 65g.

Corn & Cucumber Salad

Servings:4
Cooking Time:10 Minutes
Ingredients:
- 3 tbsp olive oil
- 3 tbsp pepitas, roasted
- 2 tbsp cilantro, chopped
- 1 cup corn
- 1 cup radishes, sliced
- 2 avocados, mashed
- 2 cucumbers, chopped
- 2 tbsp Greek yogurt
- 1 tsp balsamic vinegar
- 2 tbsp lime juice
- Salt and black pepper to taste

Directions:
1. In a bowl, whisk the olive oil, avocados, salt, pepper, lime juice, yogurt, and vinegar until smooth. Combine pepitas, cilantro, corn, radishes, and cucumbers in a salad bowl. Pour the avocado dressing over salad and toss to combine. Serve.

Nutrition Info:
- Info Per Serving: Calories: 410;Fat: 32g;Protein: 4g;Carbs: 25g.

Simple Tuna Salad

Servings:2
Cooking Time:10 Minutes
Ingredients:

- 2 tbsp olive oil
- ½ iceberg lettuce, torn
- ¼ endive, chopped
- 1 tomato, cut into wedges
- 5 oz canned tuna, flaked
- 4 black olives, sliced
- 1 tbsp lemon juice
- Salt and black pepper to taste

Directions:
1. In a salad bowl, mix olive oil, lemon juice, salt, and pepper. Add in lettuce, endive, and tuna and toss to coat. Top with black olives and tomato wedges and serve.

Nutrition Info:
- Info Per Serving: Calories: 260;Fat: 18g;Protein: 11g;Carbs: 3g.

Herby Yogurt Sauce

Servings:4
Cooking Time:5 Minutes
Ingredients:

- ¼ tsp fresh lemon juice
- 1 cup plain yogurt
- 2 tbsp fresh cilantro, minced
- 2 tbsp fresh mint, minced
- 1 garlic clove, minced
- Salt and black pepper to taste

Directions:
1. Place the lemon juice, yogurt, cilantro, mint, and garlic together in a bowl and mix well. Season with salt and pepper. Let sit for about 30 minutes to blend the flavors. Store in an airtight container in the refrigerator for up to 2-3 days.

Nutrition Info:
- Info Per Serving: Calories: 46;Fat: 0.8g;Protein: 3.6g;Carbs: 4.8g.

Bell Pepper & Roasted Cabbage Salad

Servings:4
Cooking Time:35 Minutes
Ingredients:

- 1 head green cabbage, shredded
- 4 tbsp olive oil
- 1 carrot, julienned
- ½ red bell pepper, seeded and julienned
- ½ green bell pepper, julienned
- 1 cucumber, shredded
- 1 shallot, sliced
- 2 tbsp parsley, chopped
- 1 tsp Dijon mustard
- 1 lemon, juiced
- 1 tsp mayonnaise
- Salt to taste

Directions:
1. Preheat the oven to 380 F. Season the green cabbage with salt and drizzle with some olive oil. Transfer to a baking dish and roast for 20-25 minutes, stirring often. Remove to a bowl and let cool for a few minutes. Stir in carrot, bell peppers, shallot, cucumber, and parsley. In another bowl, add the remaining olive oil, lemon juice, mustard, mayonnaise, and salt and whisk until well mixed. Drizzle over the cabbage mixture and toss to coat. Serve.

Nutrition Info:
- Info Per Serving: Calories: 195;Fat: 15g;Protein: 3.2g;Carbs: 16g.

Arugula & Fruit Salad

Servings:4
Cooking Time:5 Minutes
Ingredients:
- 6 figs, quartered
- 2 cups arugula
- 1 cup strawberries, halved
- 1 tbsp hemp seeds
- 1 cucumber, sliced
- 1 tbsp lime juice
- 1 tbsp tahini paste

Directions:
1. Spread the arugula on a serving plate. Top with strawberries, figs, and cucumber. In another bowl, whisk tahini, hemp seeds, and lime juice and pour over the salad. Serve.

Nutrition Info:
- Info Per Serving: Calories: 220;Fat: 5g;Protein: 4g;Carbs: 11g.

Leek Cream Soup With Hazelnuts

Servings:4
Cooking Time:25 Minutes
Ingredients:
- 2 tbsp olive oil
- 1 tbsp ground hazelnuts
- 4 leeks (white part), sliced
- 1 onion, chopped
- 2 garlic cloves, minced
- 4 cups chicken stock
- ¼ cup heavy cream
- 2 tbsp chopped chives

Directions:
1. Warm the olive oil in a medium saucepan. Add the leeks, garlic, and onion and sauté over low heat until tender, 3-5 minutes. Add ½ cup of chicken stock, then puree the mixture in a blender until smooth. Return the chicken stock mixture to the saucepan. Add the remaining chicken stock and simmer for 10 minutes. Stir in the heavy cream until combined. Pour into bowls and garnish with hazelnuts and chives. Serve and enjoy!

Nutrition Info:
- Info Per Serving: Calories: 395;Fat: 33.8g;Protein: 6g;Carbs: 22g.

Italian Pork Meatball Soup

Servings:4
Cooking Time:35 Minutes
Ingredients:
- 2 tbsp olive oil
- ½ cup white rice
- ½ lb ground pork
- Salt and black pepper to taste
- 2 garlic cloves, minced
- 1 onion, chopped
- ½ tsp dried thyme
- 4 cups beef stock
- ½ tsp saffron powder
- 14 oz canned tomatoes, diced
- 1 tbsp parsley, chopped

Directions:
1. In a bowl, mix ground pork, rice, salt, and pepper with your hands. Shape the mixture into ½-inch balls; set aside.
2. Warm the olive oil in a pot over medium heat and cook the onion and garlic for 5 minutes. Pour in beef stock, thyme, saffron powder, and tomatoes and bring to a boil. Add in the pork balls and cook for 20 minutes. Adjust the seasoning with salt and pepper. Serve sprinkled with parsley.

Nutrition Info:
- Info Per Serving: Calories: 380;Fat: 18g;Protein: 18g;Carbs: 29g.

Mushroom And Soba Noodle Soup

Servings:4
Cooking Time: 10 Minutes
Ingredients:
- 2 tablespoons coconut oil
- 8 ounces shiitake mushrooms, stemmed and sliced thin
- 1 tablespoon minced fresh ginger
- 4 scallions, sliced thin
- 1 garlic clove, minced
- 1 teaspoon sea salt
- 4 cups low-sodium vegetable broth
- 3 cups water
- 4 ounces soba noodles
- 1 bunch spinach, blanched, rinsed and cut into strips
- 1 tablespoon freshly squeezed lemon juice

Directions:
1. Heat the coconut oil in a stockpot over medium heat until melted.
2. Add the mushrooms, ginger, scallions, garlic, and salt. Sauté for 5 minutes or until fragrant and the mushrooms are tender.
3. Pour in the vegetable broth and water. Bring to a boil, then add the soba noodles and cook for 5 minutes or until al dente.
4. Turn off the heat and add the spinach and lemon juice. Stir to mix well.
5. Pour the soup in a large bowl and serve immediately.

Nutrition Info:
- Info Per Serving: Calories: 254;Fat: 9.2g;Protein: 13.1g;Carbs: 33.9g.

Minty Bulgur With Fried Halloumi

Servings:4
Cooking Time:35 Minutes
Ingredients:
- 2 tbsp olive oil
- 4 halloumi cheese slices
- 1 cup bulgur
- 1 cup parsley, chopped
- ¼ cup mint, chopped
- 3 tbsp lemon juice
- 1 red onion, sliced
- Salt and black pepper to taste

Directions:
1. Bring to a boil a pot of water over medium heat. Add in bulgur and simmer for 15 minutes. Drain and let it cool in a bowl. Stir in parsley, mint, lemon juice, onion, salt, and pepper. Warm half of olive oil in a pan over medium heat. Cook the halloumi for 4-5 minutes on both sides until golden. Arrange the fried cheese on top of the bulgur and serve.

Nutrition Info:
- Info Per Serving: Calories: 330;Fat: 12g;Protein: 28g;Carbs: 31g.

Fruit Salad With Sesame Seeds & Nuts

Servings:4
Cooking Time:15 Minutes
Ingredients:
- ¼ cup extra-virgin olive oil
- 2 apples, peeled and sliced
- 1 tbsp lemon juice
- 1 orange, peeled and diced
- ½ cup sliced strawberries
- ½ cup shredded coleslaw mix
- ½ cup walnut halves
- ¼ cup slivered almonds
- ¼ cup balsamic vinegar
- 2 tbsp sesame seeds
- Salt and black pepper to taste

Directions:
1. Place the apples and lemon juice in a bowl and toss to prevent browning. Add the orange, strawberries, coleslaw mix, walnuts, and almonds and toss well to mix. In a bowl, whisk together the balsamic vinegar and olive oil and season with salt and pepper. Pour the dressing over the salad and toss to coat. Top with sesame seeds and serve.

Nutrition Info:
- Info Per Serving: Calories: 299;Fat: 17g;Protein: 8g;Carbs: 44g.

Sautéed Kale With Olives

Servings:2
Cooking Time: 10 Minutes
Ingredients:
- 1 bunch kale, leaves chopped and stems minced
- ½ cup celery leaves, roughly chopped, or additional parsley
- ½ bunch flat-leaf parsley, stems and leaves roughly chopped
- 4 garlic cloves, chopped
- 2 teaspoons olive oil
- ¼ cup pitted Kalamata olives, chopped
- Grated zest and juice of 1 lemon
- Salt and pepper, to taste

Directions:
1. Place the kale, celery leaves, parsley, and garlic in a steamer basket set over a medium saucepan. Steam over medium-high heat, covered, for 15 minutes. Remove from the heat and squeeze out any excess moisture.
2. Place a large skillet over medium heat. Add the oil, then add the kale mixture to the skillet. Cook, stirring often, for 5 minutes.
3. Remove from the heat and add the olives and lemon zest and juice. Season with salt and pepper and serve.

Nutrition Info:
- Info Per Serving: Calories: 86;Fat: 6.4g;Protein: 1.8g;Carbs: 7.5g.

Cheese & Pecan Salad With Orange Dressing

Servings:2
Cooking Time:10 Minutes
Ingredients:
- Dressing
- 1 tbsp olive oil
- 2 tbsp orange juice
- 1 tbsp cider vinegar
- 1 tbsp honey
- Salt and black pepper to taste
- Salad
- 2 cups packed baby kale
- ½ small fennel bulb, sliced
- 3 tbsp toasted pecans, chopped
- 2 oz ricotta cheese, crumbled

Directions:
1. Mix the orange juice, olive oil, vinegar, and honey in a small bowl. Season with salt and pepper and set aside. Divide the baby kale, orange segments, fennel, pecans, and ricotta cheese evenly between two plates. Drizzle half of the dressing over each salad.

Nutrition Info:
- Info Per Serving: Calories: 502;Fat: 39g;Protein: 13g;Carbs: 31g.

Bean & Squash Soup

Servings:4
Cooking Time:55 Minutes
Ingredients:
- 2 tbsp olive oil
- 1 yellow onion, chopped
- 2 garlic cloves, minced
- 1 carrot, chopped
- 1 zucchini, chopped
- 1 squash, peeled and cubed
- 2 tbsp parsley, chopped
- ¼ fennel bulb, chopped
- 30 oz canned cannellini beans
- 2 cups veggie stock
- ¼ tsp dried thyme
- Salt and black pepper to taste
- 1 cup green beans
- ¼ cup Parmesan, grated

Directions:
1. Warm the olive oil in a pot over medium heat and cook onion, garlic, carrot, squash, zucchini, and fennel for 5 minutes. Stir in cannellini beans, veggie stock, 4 cups of water, thyme, salt, and pepper and bring to a boil; cook for 10 minutes. Put in green beans and cook for another 10 minutes. Serve sprinkled with Parmesan cheese and parsley.

Nutrition Info:
- Info Per Serving: Calories: 310;Fat: 12g;Protein: 11g;Carbs: 18g.

Picante Avocado Salad With Anchovies

Servings:4
Cooking Time:10 Minutes
Ingredients:
- 3 tbsp olive oil
- 2 avocados, diced
- 2 bell peppers, sliced
- 1 jalapeño pepper, minced
- ½ cup red onion, thinly sliced
- 1 ripe tomato, chopped
- 2 pickles, sliced
- 2 oz anchovies fillets, flaked
- 1 cup arugula
- 1 tbsp red wine vinegar
- 1 tbsp fresh lemon juice
- ½ tsp chili flakes
- ¼ tsp oregano
- ½ tsp sage
- Salt and black pepper to taste

Directions:
1. In a bowl, combine the bell peppers, jalapeño pepper, onion, tomato, pickles, anchovies, avocados, and arugula. In another bowl, mix the vinegar, lemon juice, olive oil, oregano, sage, chili flakes, salt, and black pepper. Pour over the salad and toss to coat. Serve chilled.

Nutrition Info:
- Info Per Serving: Calories: 330;Fat: 31g;Protein: 3.1g;Carbs: 16g.

Cabbage & Turkey Soup

Servings:4
Cooking Time:40 Minutes
Ingredients:
- 2 tbsp olive oil
- ½ lb turkey breast, cubed
- 2 leeks, sliced
- 4 spring onions, chopped
- 2 cups green cabbage, grated
- 4 celery sticks, chopped
- 4 cups vegetable stock
- ½ tsp sweet paprika
- ½ tsp ground nutmeg
- Salt and black pepper to taste

Directions:
1. Warm the olive oil in a pot over medium heat and brown turkey for 4 minutes, stirring occasionally. Add in leeks, spring onions, and celery and cook for another minute. Stir in cabbage, vegetable stock, sweet paprika, nutmeg, salt, and pepper and bring to a boil. Cook for 30 minutes. Serve.

Nutrition Info:
- Info Per Serving: Calories: 320;Fat: 16g;Protein: 19g;Carbs: 25g.

Vegetable Mains And Meatless Recipes

Brussels Sprouts Linguine

Servings:4
Cooking Time: 25 Minutes
Ingredients:
- 8 ounces whole-wheat linguine
- ⅓ cup plus 2 tablespoons extra-virgin olive oil, divided
- 1 medium sweet onion, diced
- 2 to 3 garlic cloves, smashed
- 8 ounces Brussels sprouts, chopped
- ½ cup chicken stock
- ⅓ cup dry white wine
- ½ cup shredded Parmesan cheese
- 1 lemon, quartered

Directions:
1. Bring a large pot of water to a boil and cook the pasta for about 5 minutes, or until al dente. Drain the pasta and reserve 1 cup of the pasta water. Mix the cooked pasta with 2 tablespoons of the olive oil. Set aside.
2. In a large skillet, heat the remaining ⅓ cup of the olive oil over medium heat. Add the onion to the skillet and sauté for about 4 minutes, or until tender. Add the smashed garlic cloves and sauté for 1 minute, or until fragrant.
3. Stir in the Brussels sprouts and cook covered for 10 minutes. Pour in the chicken stock to prevent burning. Once the Brussels sprouts have wilted and are fork-tender, add white wine and cook for about 5 minutes, or until reduced.
4. Add the pasta to the skillet and add the pasta water as needed.
5. Top with the Parmesan cheese and squeeze the lemon over the dish right before eating.

Nutrition Info:
- Info Per Serving: Calories: 502;Fat: 31.0g;Protein: 15.0g;Carbs: 50.0g.

Artichoke & Bean Pot

Servings:4
Cooking Time:40 Minutes
Ingredients:
- 2 tbsp olive oil
- 10 artichoke hearts, halved
- 1 onion, sliced
- 12 whole baby carrots
- ½ cup chopped celery
- 1 lemon, juiced
- 2 tbsp chopped fresh basil
- 1 red chili, sliced
- ¾ cup frozen fava beans
- Salt and black pepper to taste

Directions:
1. Warm olive oil in a pot over medium heat and sauté onion, carrots, and celery for 7-8 minutes until tender. Stir in lemon juice, butter, and 1 cup of water. Bring to a boil, then lower the heat and simmer for 10-15 minutes. Add in artichoke hearts, fava beans, salt, and pepper and cook covered for another 10 minutes. Top with basil and red chili and serve.

Nutrition Info:
- Info Per Serving: Calories: 353;Fat: 4.1g;Protein: 22g;Carbs: 68g.

Veggie Rice Bowls With Pesto Sauce

Servings: 2
Cooking Time: 1 Minute

Ingredients:

- 2 cups water
- 1 cup arborio rice, rinsed
- Salt and ground black pepper, to taste
- 2 eggs
- 1 cup broccoli florets
- ½ pound Brussels sprouts
- 1 carrot, peeled and chopped
- 1 small beet, peeled and cubed
- ¼ cup pesto sauce
- Lemon wedges, for serving

Directions:

1. Combine the water, rice, salt, and pepper in the Instant Pot. Insert a trivet over rice and place a steamer basket on top. Add the eggs, broccoli, Brussels sprouts, carrots, beet cubes, salt, and pepper to the steamer basket.
2. Lock the lid. Select the Manual mode and set the cooking time for 1 minute at High Pressure.
3. When the timer beeps, perform a natural pressure release for 10 minutes, then release any remaining pressure. Carefully open the lid.
4. Remove the steamer basket and trivet from the pot and transfer the eggs to a bowl of ice water. Peel and halve the eggs. Use a fork to fluff the rice.
5. Divide the rice, broccoli, Brussels sprouts, carrot, beet cubes, and eggs into two bowls. Top with a dollop of pesto sauce and serve with the lemon wedges.

Nutrition Info:

- Info Per Serving: Calories: 590;Fat: 34.1g;Protein: 21.9g;Carbs: 50.0g.

Spicy Kale With Almonds

Servings: 4
Cooking Time: 25 Minutes

Ingredients:

- 2 tbsp olive oil
- ¼ cup slivered almonds
- 1 lb chopped kale
- ¼ cup vegetable broth
- 1 lemon, juiced and zested
- 1 garlic clove, minced
- 1 tbsp red pepper flakes
- Salt and black pepper to taste

Directions:

1. Warm olive oil in a pan over medium heat and sauté garlic, kale, salt, and pepper for 8-9 minutes until soft. Add in lemon juice, lemon zest, red pepper flakes, and vegetable broth and continue cooking until the liquid evaporates, about 3-5 minutes. Garnish with almonds and serve.

Nutrition Info:

- Info Per Serving: Calories: 123;Fat: 8.1g;Protein: 4g;Carbs: 10.8g.

Veggie-stuffed Portabello Mushrooms

Servings:6
Cooking Time: 24 To 25 Minutes

Ingredients:

- 3 tablespoons extra-virgin olive oil, divided
- 1 cup diced onion
- 2 garlic cloves, minced
- 1 large zucchini, diced
- 3 cups chopped mushrooms
- 1 cup chopped tomato
- 1 teaspoon dried oregano
- ¼ teaspoon kosher salt
- ¼ teaspoon crushed red pepper
- 6 large portabello mushrooms, stems and gills removed
- Cooking spray
- 4 ounces fresh Mozzarella cheese, shredded

Directions:

1. In a large skillet over medium heat, heat 2 tablespoons of the oil. Add the onion and sauté for 4 minutes. Stir in the garlic and sauté for 1 minute.
2. Stir in the zucchini, mushrooms, tomato, oregano, salt and red pepper. Cook for 10 minutes, stirring constantly. Remove from the heat.
3. Meanwhile, heat a grill pan over medium-high heat.
4. Brush the remaining 1 tablespoon of the oil over the portabello mushroom caps. Place the mushrooms, bottom-side down, on the grill pan. Cover with a sheet of aluminum foil sprayed with nonstick cooking spray. Cook for 5 minutes.
5. Flip the mushroom caps over, and spoon about ½ cup of the cooked vegetable mixture into each cap. Top each with about 2½ tablespoons of the Mozzarella.
6. Cover and grill for 4 to 5 minutes, or until the cheese is melted.
7. Using a spatula, transfer the portabello mushrooms to a plate. Let cool for about 5 minutes before serving.

Nutrition Info:

- Info Per Serving: Calories: 111;Fat: 4.0g;Protein: 11.0g;Carbs: 11.0g.

Baked Potato With Veggie Mix

Servings:4
Cooking Time:45 Minutes

Ingredients:

- 4 tbsp olive oil
- 1 lb potatoes, peeled and diced
- 2 red bell peppers, halved
- 1 lb mushrooms, sliced
- 2 tomatoes, diced
- 8 garlic cloves, peeled
- 1 eggplant, sliced
- 1 yellow onion, quartered
- ½ tsp dried oregano
- ¼ tsp caraway seeds
- Salt to taste

Directions:

1. Preheat the oven to 390 F. In a bowl, combine the bell peppers, mushrooms, tomatoes, eggplant, onion, garlic, salt, olive oil, oregano, and caraway seeds. Set aside. Arrange the potatoes on a baking dish and bake for 15 minutes. Top with the veggies mixture and bake for 15-20 minutes until tender.

Nutrition Info:

- Info Per Serving: Calories: 302;Fat: 15g;Protein: 8.5g;Carbs: 39g.

Grilled Vegetable Skewers

Servings:4
Cooking Time: 10 Minutes
Ingredients:
- 4 medium red onions, peeled and sliced into 6 wedges
- 4 medium zucchini, cut into 1-inch-thick slices
- 2 beefsteak tomatoes, cut into quarters
- 4 red bell peppers, cut into 2-inch squares
- 2 orange bell peppers, cut into 2-inch squares
- 2 yellow bell peppers, cut into 2-inch squares
- 2 tablespoons plus 1 teaspoon olive oil, divided
- SPECIAL EQUIPMENT:
- 4 wooden skewers, soaked in water for at least 30 minutes

Directions:
1. Preheat the grill to medium-high heat.
2. Skewer the vegetables by alternating between red onion, zucchini, tomatoes, and the different colored bell peppers. Brush them with 2 tablespoons of olive oil.
3. Oil the grill grates with 1 teaspoon of olive oil and grill the vegetable skewers for 5 minutes. Flip the skewers and grill for 5 minutes more, or until they are cooked to your liking.
4. Let the skewers cool for 5 minutes before serving.

Nutrition Info:
- Info Per Serving: Calories: 115;Fat: 3.0g;Protein: 3.5g;Carbs: 18.7g.

Grilled Za´atar Zucchini Rounds

Servings:4
Cooking Time:20 Minutes
Ingredients:
- 2 tbsp olive oil
- 4 zucchinis, sliced
- 1 tbsp za'atar seasoning
- Salt to taste
- 2 tbsp parsley, chopped

Directions:
1. Preheat the grill on high. Cut the zucchini lengthways into ½-inch thin pieces. Brush the zucchini 'steaks' with olive oil and season with salt and za'atar seasoning. Grill for 6 minutes on both sides. Sprinkle with parsley and serve.

Nutrition Info:
- Info Per Serving: Calories: 91;Fat: 7.4g;Protein: 2.4g;Carbs: 6.6g.

Chili Vegetable Skillet

Servings:4
Cooking Time:30 Minutes
Ingredients:
- 1 cup condensed cream of mushroom soup
- 1 ½ lb eggplants, cut into chunks
- 1 cup cremini mushrooms, sliced
- 4 tbsp olive oil
- 1 carrot, thinly sliced
- 1 can tomatoes
- ½ cup red onion, thinly sliced
- 2 garlic cloves, minced
- 1 tsp fresh rosemary
- 1 tsp chili pepper
- Salt and black pepper to taste
- 2 tbsp parsley, chopped
- ¼ cup Parmesan cheese, grated

Directions:
1. Warm the olive oil in a skillet over medium heat. Add in the eggplant and cook until golden brown on all sides, about 5 minutes; set aside. Add in the carrot, onion, and mushrooms and sauté for 4 more minutes to the same skillet. Add in garlic, rosemary, and chili pepper. Cook for another 30-40 seconds. Add in 1 cup of water, cream of mushroom soup, and tomatoes. Bring to a boil and lower the heat; simmer covered for 5 minutes. Mix in sautéed eggplants and parsley and cook for 10 more minutes. Sprinkle with salt and black pepper. Serve topped with Parmesan cheese.

Nutrition Info:
- Info Per Serving: Calories: 261;Fat: 18.7g;Protein: 5g;Carbs: 23g.

Cauliflower Hash With Carrots

Servings:4
Cooking Time: 10 Minutes
Ingredients:
- 3 tablespoons extra-virgin olive oil
- 1 large onion, chopped
- 1 tablespoon minced garlic
- 2 cups diced carrots
- 4 cups cauliflower florets
- ½ teaspoon ground cumin
- 1 teaspoon salt

Directions:
1. In a large skillet, heat the olive oil over medium heat.
2. Add the onion and garlic and sauté for 1 minute. Stir in the carrots and stir-fry for 3 minutes.
3. Add the cauliflower florets, cumin, and salt and toss to combine.
4. Cover and cook for 3 minutes until lightly browned. Stir well and cook, uncovered, for 3 to 4 minutes, until softened.
5. Remove from the heat and serve warm.

Nutrition Info:
- Info Per Serving: Calories: 158;Fat: 10.8g;Protein: 3.1g;Carbs: 14.9g.

Garlicky Broccoli Rabe

Servings: 4
Cooking Time: 5 To 6 Minutes
Ingredients:
- 14 ounces broccoli rabe, trimmed and cut into 1-inch pieces
- 2 teaspoons salt, plus more for seasoning
- Black pepper, to taste
- 2 tablespoons extra-virgin olive oil
- 3 garlic cloves, minced
- ¼ teaspoon red pepper flakes

Directions:
1. Bring 3 quarts water to a boil in a large saucepan. Add the broccoli rabe and 2 teaspoons of the salt to the boiling water and cook for 2 to 3 minutes, or until wilted and tender.
2. Drain the broccoli rabe. Transfer to ice water and let sit until chilled. Drain again and pat dry.
3. In a skillet over medium heat, heat the oil and add the garlic and red pepper flakes. Sauté for about 2 minutes, or until the garlic begins to sizzle.
4. Increase the heat to medium-high. Stir in the broccoli rabe and cook for about 1 minute, or until heated through, stirring constantly. Season with salt and pepper.
5. Serve immediately.

Nutrition Info:
- Info Per Serving: Calories: 87;Fat: 7.3g;Protein: 3.4g;Carbs: 4.0g.

Cauliflower Rice Risotto With Mushrooms

Servings: 4
Cooking Time: 10 Minutes
Ingredients:
- 1 teaspoon extra-virgin olive oil
- ½ cup chopped portobello mushrooms
- 4 cups cauliflower rice
- ½ cup half-and-half
- ¼ cup low-sodium vegetable broth
- 1 cup shredded Parmesan cheese

Directions:
1. In a medium skillet, heat the olive oil over medium-low heat until shimmering.
2. Add the mushrooms and stir-fry for 3 minutes.
3. Stir in the cauliflower rice, half-and-half, and vegetable broth. Cover and bring to a boil over high heat for 5 minutes, stirring occasionally.
4. Add the Parmesan cheese and stir to combine. Continue cooking for an additional 3 minutes until the cheese is melted.
5. Divide the mixture into four bowls and serve warm.

Nutrition Info:
- Info Per Serving: Calories: 167;Fat: 10.7g;Protein: 12.1g;Carbs: 8.1g.

Chickpea Lettuce Wraps With Celery

Servings: 4
Cooking Time: 0 Minutes
Ingredients:
- 1 can low-sodium chickpeas, drained and rinsed
- 1 celery stalk, thinly sliced
- 2 tablespoons finely chopped red onion
- 2 tablespoons unsalted tahini
- 3 tablespoons honey mustard
- 1 tablespoon capers, undrained
- 12 butter lettuce leaves

Directions:
1. In a bowl, mash the chickpeas with a potato masher or the back of a fork until mostly smooth.
2. Add the celery, red onion, tahini, honey mustard, and capers to the bowl and stir until well incorporated.
3. For each serving, place three overlapping lettuce leaves on a plate and top with ¼ of the mashed chickpea filling, then roll up. Repeat with the remaining lettuce leaves and chickpea mixture.

Nutrition Info:
- Info Per Serving: Calories: 182;Fat: 7.1g;Protein: 10.3g;Carbs: 19.6g.

Eggplant Rolls In Tomato Sauce

Servings:4
Cooking Time:60 Minutes

Ingredients:

- 2 tbsp olive oil
- 1 ½ cups ricotta cheese
- 2 cans diced tomatoes
- 1 shallot, finely chopped
- 2 garlic cloves, minced
- 1 tbsp Italian seasoning
- 1 tsp dried oregano
- 2 eggplants
- ½ cup grated mozzarella
- Salt to taste
- ¼ tsp red pepper flakes

Directions:

1. Preheat oven to 350 F. Warm olive oil in a pot over medium heat and sauté shallot and garlic for 3 minutes until tender and fragrant. Mix in tomatoes, oregano, Italian seasoning, salt, and red flakes and simmer for 6 minutes.
2. Cut the eggplants lengthwise into 1,5-inch slices and season with salt. Grill them for 2-3 minutes per side until softened. Place them on a plate and spoon 2 tbsp of ricotta cheese. Wrap them and arrange on a greased baking dish. Pour over the sauce and scatter with the mozzarella cheese. Bake for 15-20 minutes until golden-brown and bubbling.

Nutrition Info:

- Info Per Serving: Calories: 362;Fat: 17g;Protein: 19g;Carbs: 38g.

Roasted Vegetable Medley

Servings:2
Cooking Time:65 Minutes

Ingredients:

- 1 head garlic, cloves split apart, unpeeled
- 3 tbsp olive oil
- 2 carrots, cut into strips
- ¼ lb asparagus, chopped
- ½ lb Brussels sprouts, halved
- 2 cups broccoli florets
- 1 cup cherry tomatoes
- ½ fresh lemon, sliced
- Salt and black pepper to taste

Directions:

1. Preheat oven to 375 F. Drizzle the garlic cloves with some olive oil and lightly wrap them in a small piece of foil. Place the packet in the oven and roast for 30 minutes. Place all the vegetables and the lemon slices into a large mixing bowl. Drizzle with the remaining olive oil and season with salt and pepper. Increase the oven to 400 F. Pour the vegetables on a sheet pan in a single layer, leaving the packet of garlic cloves on the pan. Roast for 20 minutes, shaking occasionally until tender. Remove the pan from the oven. Let the garlic cloves sit until cool enough to handle, then remove the skins. Top the vegetables with roasted garlic and serve.

Nutrition Info:

- Info Per Serving: Calories: 256;Fat: 15g;Protein: 7g;Carbs: 31g.

Chargrilled Vegetable Kebabs

Servings:4
Cooking Time:26 Minutes
Ingredients:
- 2 red bell peppers, cut into squares
- 2 zucchinis, sliced into half-moons
- 6 portobello mushroom caps, quartered
- ¼ cup olive oil
- 1 tsp Dijon mustard
- 1 tsp fresh rosemary, chopped
- 1 garlic clove, minced
- Salt and black pepper to taste
- 2 red onions, cut into wedges

Directions:
1. Preheat your grill to High. Mix the olive oil, mustard, rosemary, garlic, salt, and pepper in a bowl. Reserve half of the oil mixture for serving. Thread the vegetables in alternating order onto metal skewers and brush them with the remaining oil mixture. Grill them for about 15 minutes until browned, turning occasionally. Transfer the kebabs to a serving platter and remove the skewers. Drizzle with reserved oil mixture and serve.

Nutrition Info:
- Info Per Serving: Calories: 96;Fat: 9.2g;Protein: 1.1g;Carbs: 3.6g.

Italian Hot Green Beans

Servings:4
Cooking Time:25 Minutes
Ingredients:
- 2 tbsp olive oil
- 1 red bell pepper, diced
- 1 ½ lb green beans
- 4 garlic cloves, minced
- ½ tsp mustard seeds
- ½ tsp fennel seeds
- 1 tsp dried dill weed
- 2 tomatoes, chopped
- 1 cup cream of celery soup
- 1 tsp Italian herb mix
- 1 tsp chili powder
- Salt and black pepper to taste

Directions:
1. Warm the olive oil in a saucepan over medium heat. Add and fry the bell pepper and green beans for about 5 minutes, stirring periodically to promote even cooking. Add in the garlic, mustard seeds, fennel seeds, and dill and continue sautéing for an additional 1 minute or until fragrant. Add in the pureed tomatoes, cream of celery soup, Italian herb mix, chili powder, salt, and black pepper. Continue to simmer, covered, for 10-12 minutes until the green beans are tender.

Nutrition Info:
- Info Per Serving: Calories: 160;Fat: 9g;Protein: 5g;Carbs: 19g.

Celery And Mustard Greens

Servings: 4
Cooking Time: 15 Minutes

Ingredients:
- ½ cup low-sodium vegetable broth
- 1 celery stalk, roughly chopped
- ½ sweet onion, chopped
- ½ large red bell pepper, thinly sliced
- 2 garlic cloves, minced
- 1 bunch mustard greens, roughly chopped

Directions:
1. Pour the vegetable broth into a large cast iron pan and bring it to a simmer over medium heat.
2. Stir in the celery, onion, bell pepper, and garlic. Cook uncovered for about 3 to 5 minutes, or until the onion is softened.
3. Add the mustard greens to the pan and stir well. Cover, reduce the heat to low, and cook for an additional 10 minutes, or until the liquid is evaporated and the greens are wilted.
4. Remove from the heat and serve warm.

Nutrition Info:
- Info Per Serving: Calories: 39;Fat: 0g;Protein: 3.1g;Carbs: 6.8g.

Easy Zucchini Patties

Servings: 2
Cooking Time: 5 Minutes

Ingredients:
- 2 medium zucchinis, shredded
- 1 teaspoon salt, divided
- 2 eggs
- 2 tablespoons chickpea flour
- 1 tablespoon chopped fresh mint
- 1 scallion, chopped
- 2 tablespoons extra-virgin olive oil

Directions:
1. Put the shredded zucchini in a fine-mesh strainer and season with ½ teaspoon of salt. Set aside.
2. Beat together the eggs, chickpea flour, mint, scallion, and remaining ½ teaspoon of salt in a medium bowl.
3. Squeeze the zucchini to drain as much liquid as possible. Add the zucchini to the egg mixture and stir until well incorporated.
4. Heat the olive oil in a large skillet over medium-high heat.
5. Drop the zucchini mixture by spoonful into the skillet. Gently flatten the zucchini with the back of a spatula.
6. Cook for 2 to 3 minutes or until golden brown. Flip and cook for an additional 2 minutes.
7. Remove from the heat and serve on a plate.

Nutrition Info:
- Info Per Serving: Calories: 264;Fat: 20.0g;Protein: 9.8g;Carbs: 16.1g.

Simple Oven-baked Green Beans

Servings: 6
Cooking Time: 15 Minutes

Ingredients:
- 2 tbsp olive oil
- 2 lb green beans, trimmed
- Salt and black pepper to taste

Directions:
1. Preheat oven to 400 F. Toss the green beans with some olive oil, salt, and spread them in a single layer on a greased baking dish. Roast for 8-10 minutes. Transfer green beans to a serving platter and drizzle with the remaining olive oil.

Nutrition Info:
- Info Per Serving: Calories: 157;Fat: 2g;Protein: 3g;Carbs: 6g.

Homemade Vegetarian Moussaka

Servings: 4
Cooking Time: 80 Minutes

Ingredients:
- 2 tbsp olive oil
- 1 yellow onion, chopped
- 2 garlic cloves, chopped
- 2 eggplants, halved
- ½ cup vegetable broth
- Salt and black pepper to taste
- ½ tsp paprika
- ¼ cup parsley, chopped
- 1 tsp basil, chopped
- 1 tsp hot sauce
- 1 tomato, chopped
- 2 tbsp tomato puree
- 6 Kalamata olives, chopped
- ½ cup feta cheese, crumbled

Directions:
1. Preheat oven to 360 F. Remove the tender center part of the eggplants and chop it. Arrange the eggplant halves on a baking tray and drizzle with some olive oil. Roast for 35-40 minutes.
2. Warm the remaining olive oil in a skillet over medium heat and add eggplant flesh, onion, and garlic and sauté for 5 minutes until tender. Stir in the vegetable broth, salt, pepper, basil, hot sauce, paprika, tomato, and tomato puree. Lower the heat and simmer for 10-15 minutes. Once the eggplants are ready, remove them from the oven and fill them with the mixture. Top with Kalamata olives and feta cheese. Return to the oven and bake for 10-15 minutes. Sprinkle with parsley.

Nutrition Info:
- Info Per Serving: Calories: 223;Fat: 14g;Protein: 6.9g;Carbs: 23g.

Pea & Carrot Noodles

Servings: 4
Cooking Time: 25 Minutes

Ingredients:
- 2 tbsp olive oil
- 4 carrots, spiralized
- 1 sweet onion, chopped
- 2 cups peas
- 2 garlic cloves, minced
- ¼ cup chopped fresh parsley
- Salt and black pepper to taste

Directions:
1. Warm 2 tbsp of olive oil in a pot over medium heat and sauté the onion and garlic for 3 minutes until just tender and fragrant. Add in spiralized carrots and cook for 4 minutes. Mix in peas, salt, and pepper and cook for 4 minutes. Drizzle with the remaining olive oil and sprinkle with parsley.

Nutrition Info:
- Info Per Serving: Calories: 157;Fat: 7g;Protein: 4.8g;Carbs: 19.6g.

Grilled Eggplant "steaks" With Sauce

Servings:6
Cooking Time:20 Minutes
Ingredients:
- 2 lb eggplants, sliced lengthways
- 6 tbsp olive oil
- 5 garlic cloves, minced
- 1 tsp dried oregano
- ½ tsp red pepper flakes
- ½ cup Greek yogurt
- 3 tbsp chopped fresh parsley
- 1 tsp grated lemon zest
- 2 tsp lemon juice
- 1 tsp ground cumin
- Salt and black pepper to taste

Directions:
1. In a bowl, whisk half of the olive oil, yogurt, parsley, lemon zest and juice, cumin, and salt; set aside until ready to serve. Preheat your grill to High. Rub the eggplant steaks with the remaining olive oil, oregano, salt, and pepper. Grill them for 4-6 minutes per side until browned and tender; transfer to a serving platter. Drizzle yogurt sauce over eggplant.

Nutrition Info:
- Info Per Serving: Calories: 112;Fat: 7g;Protein: 2.6g;Carbs: 11.3g.

Cauliflower Cakes With Goat Cheese

Servings:4
Cooking Time:50 Minutes
Ingredients:
- ¼ cup olive oil
- 10 oz cauliflower florets
- 1 tsp ground turmeric
- 1 tsp ground coriander
- Salt and black pepper to taste
- ½ tsp ground mustard seeds
- 4 oz Goat cheese, softened
- 2 scallions, sliced thin
- 1 large egg, lightly beaten
- 2 garlic cloves, minced
- 1 tsp grated lemon zest
- 4 lemon wedges
- ¼ cup flour

Directions:
1. Preheat oven to 420 F. In a bowl, whisk 1 tablespoon oil, turmeric, coriander, salt, ground mustard, and pepper. Add in the cauliflower and toss to coat. Transfer to a greased baking sheet and spread it in a single layer. Roast for 20-25 minutes until cauliflower is well browned and tender. Transfer the cauliflower to a large bowl and mash it coarsely with a potato masher. Stir in Goat cheese, scallions, egg, garlic, and lemon zest until well combined. Sprinkle flour over cauliflower mixture and stir to incorporate. Shape the mixture into 10-12 cakes and place them on a sheet pan. Chill to firm, about 30 minutes. Warm the remaining olive oil in a skillet over medium heat. Fry the cakes for 5-6 minutes on each side until deep golden brown and crisp. Serve with lemon wedges.

Nutrition Info:
- Info Per Serving: Calories: 320;Fat: 25g;Protein: 13g;Carbs: 12g.

Ratatouille

Servings:4
Cooking Time: 30 Minutes

Ingredients:

- 4 tablespoons extra-virgin olive oil, divided
- 1 cup diced zucchini
- 2 cups diced eggplant
- 1 cup diced onion
- 1 cup chopped green bell pepper
- 1 can no-salt-added diced tomatoes
- ½ teaspoon garlic powder
- 1 teaspoon ground thyme
- Salt and freshly ground black pepper, to taste

Directions:

1. Heat 2 tablespoons of olive oil in a large saucepan over medium heat until it shimmers.
2. Add the zucchini and eggplant and sauté for 10 minutes, stirring occasionally. If necessary, add the remaining olive oil.
3. Stir in the onion and bell pepper and sauté for 5 minutes until softened.
4. Add the diced tomatoes with their juice, garlic powder, and thyme and stir to combine. Continue cooking for 15 minutes until the vegetables are cooked through, stirring occasionally. Sprinkle with salt and black pepper.
5. Remove from the heat and serve on a plate.

Nutrition Info:

- Info Per Serving: Calories: 189;Fat: 13.7g;Protein: 3.1g;Carbs: 14.8g.

Tahini & Feta Butternut Squash

Servings:6
Cooking Time:50 Minutes

Ingredients:

- 3 lb butternut squash, peeled, halved lengthwise, and seeded
- 3 tbsp olive oil
- Salt and black pepper to taste
- 2 tbsp fresh thyme, chopped
- 1 tbsp tahini
- 1 ½ tsp lemon juice
- 1 tsp honey
- 1 oz feta cheese, crumbled
- ¼ cup pistachios, chopped

Directions:

1. Preheat oven to 425 F. Slice the squash halves crosswise into ½-inch-thick pieces. Toss them with 2 tablespoons of olive oil, salt, and pepper and arrange them on a greased baking sheet in an even layer. Roast for 45-50 minutes or until golden and tender. Transfer squash to a serving platter. Whisk tahini, lemon juice, honey, remaining oil, and salt together in a bowl. Drizzle squash with tahini dressing and sprinkle with feta, pistachios, and thyme. Serve and enjoy!

Nutrition Info:

- Info Per Serving: Calories: 212;Fat: 12g;Protein: 4.1g;Carbs: 27g.

Poultry And Meats Recipes

Rosemary Pork Chops With Cabbage Mix

Servings:4
Cooking Time:35 Minutes
Ingredients:
- ½ green cabbage head, shredded
- 2 tsp olive oil
- 4 pork chops
- 4 bell peppers, chopped
- 1 tsp rosemary
- 2 tbsp wine vinegar
- 2 spring onions, chopped
- Salt and black pepper to taste

Directions:
1. Warm half of oil in a skillet over medium heat. Cook spring onions for 3 minutes. Stir in vinegar, cabbage, bell peppers, salt, and pepper and simmer for 10 minutes. Heat off.
2. Preheat the grill over medium heat. Sprinkle pork chops with remaining oil, salt, pepper, and rosemary and grill for 10 minutes on both sides. Share chops into plates with cabbage mixture on the side. Serve immediately.

Nutrition Info:
- Info Per Serving: Calories: 230;Fat: 19g;Protein: 13g;Carbs: 18g.

Herby Beef Soup

Servings:4
Cooking Time:60 Minutes
Ingredients:
- 2 tbsp olive oil
- ½ lb beef stew meat, cubed
- 1 celery stalk, chopped
- 1 tsp fennel seeds
- 1 tsp hot paprika
- 1 carrot, chopped
- 1 onion, chopped
- Salt and black pepper to taste
- 2 garlic cloves, chopped
- 4 cups beef stock
- ½ tsp dried cilantro
- 1 tsp dried oregano
- 14 oz canned tomatoes, diced
- 2 tbsp parsley, chopped

Directions:
1. Warm the olive oil in a pot over medium heat and cook beef meat, onion, and garlic for 10 minutes. Stir in celery, carrots, fennel seeds, paprika, salt, pepper, cilantro, and oregano for 3 minutes. Pour in beef stock and tomatoes and bring to a boil. Cook for 40 minutes. Top with parsley.

Nutrition Info:
- Info Per Serving: Calories: 350;Fat: 16g;Protein: 38g;Carbs: 16g.

Chicken Sausage & Zucchini Soup

Servings: 4
Cooking Time: 30 Minutes
Ingredients:
- 2 tbsp olive oil
- 2 chicken sausage, chopped
- 4 cups chicken stock
- 3 garlic cloves, minced
- 1 yellow onion, chopped
- 4 zucchinis, cubed
- 1 lemon, zested
- ½ cup basil, chopped
- Salt and black pepper to taste

Directions:
1. Warm the olive oil in a pot over medium heat and brown the sausages for 5 minutes; reserve. Add zucchini, onion, and garlic to the pot and sauté for 5 minutes. Add in the chicken stock, lemon zest, salt, and pepper and bring to a boil. Simmer for 10 minutes. Return the sausages and cook for another 5 minutes. Top with basil and serve right away.

Nutrition Info:
- Info Per Serving: Calories: 280;Fat: 12g;Protein: 5g;Carbs: 17g.

Chicken Thighs With Roasted Artichokes

Servings: 4
Cooking Time: 25 Minutes
Ingredients:
- 2 artichoke hearts, halved lengthwise
- 2 tbsp butter, melted
- 3 tbsp olive oil
- 2 lemons, zested and juiced
- ½ tsp salt
- 4 chicken thighs

Directions:
1. Preheat oven to 450 F. Place a large, rimmed baking sheet in the oven. Whisk the olive oil, lemon zest, and lemon juice in a bowl. Add the artichoke hearts and turn them to coat on all sides. Lay the artichoke halves flat-side down in the center of 4 aluminum foil sheets and close up loosely to create packets. Put the chicken in the remaining lemon mixture and toss to coat. Carefully remove the hot baking sheet from the oven and pour on the butter; tilt the pan to coat.
2. Arrange the chicken thighs, skin-side down, on the sheet, add the artichoke packets. Roast for about 20 minutes or until the chicken is cooked through and the skin is slightly charred. Check the artichokes for doneness and bake for another 5 minutes if needed. Serve and enjoy!

Nutrition Info:
- Info Per Serving: Calories: 832;Fat: 80g;Protein: 19g;Carbs: 11g.

Mushroom Chicken Piccata

Servings:4
Cooking Time:25 Minutes
Ingredients:
- 3 tbsp olive oil
- 2 tbsp butter
- 1 lb chicken breasts, sliced
- Salt and black pepper to taste
- ¼ cup ground flaxseed
- 2 tbsp almond flour
- 2 cups mushrooms, sliced
- ½ cup white wine
- ¼ cup lemon juice
- ¼ cup capers, chopped
- ¼ cup parsley, chopped
- 16 oz cooked spaghetti

Directions:
1. Combine the ground flaxseed, almond flour, salt, and pepper in a bowl. Coat the chicken with the mixture.
2. Warm the olive oil in a large skillet over medium heat. Sear the chicken for 3-4 minutes per side until golden; reserve. Add the butter to the skillet and sauté the mushrooms and for 5-7 minutes. Pour in the white wine, lemon juice, capers, and salt and bring to a boil, whisking to incorporate any little browned bits that have stuck to the bottom of the skillet. Lower the heat to low and return the browned chicken. Cover and simmer 5-6 more minutes until the sauce thickens. Place the spaghetti in a serving platter and spoon the chicken and mushrooms on top. Garnish with parsley.

Nutrition Info:
- Info Per Serving: Calories: 538;Fat: 44g;Protein: 30g;Carbs: 8g.

Apricot Chicken Rice Bowls

Servings:4
Cooking Time:30 Minutes
Ingredients:
- 2 cups cooked chicken breasts, chopped
- ½ cup dried apricots, chopped
- 2 cups peeled and chopped cucumber
- 2 tbsp chicken broth
- 1 cup instant brown rice
- ¼ cup tahini
- ¼ cup Greek yogurt
- 2 tbsp scallions, chopped
- 1 tbsp lemon juice
- 1 tsp ground cumin
- ¾ tsp ground cinnamon
- ¼ tsp kosher or sea salt
- 4 tsp sesame seeds
- 1 tbsp fresh mint leaves

Directions:
1. Place the broth in a pot over medium heat and bring to a boil. Reduce the heat and add the brown rice cook. Simmer for 10 minutes or until rice is cooked through. In a bowl, mix the tahini, yogurt, scallions, lemon juice, 1 tbsp of water, cumin, cinnamon, and salt. Transfer half the tahini mixture to another medium bowl. Mix the chicken into the first bowl. When the rice is done, place it into the second bowl of tahini. Divide the chicken between 4 bowls. Spoon the rice mixture next to the chicken. Next to the chicken, place the dried apricots, and in the remaining empty section, add the cucumbers. Sprinkle with sesame seeds and fresh mint.

Nutrition Info:
- Info Per Serving: Calories: 335;Fat: 11g;Protein: 31g;Carbs: 30g.

Spanish Chicken Skillet

Servings:4
Cooking Time:25 Minutes
Ingredients:
- 2 tbsp olive oil
- ½ cup chicken stock
- 4 chicken breasts
- 2 garlic cloves, minced
- 1 celery stalk, chopped
- 1 tbsp oregano, dried
- Salt and black pepper to taste
- 1 white onion, chopped
- 1 ½ cups tomatoes, cubed
- 10 green olives, sliced

Directions:
1. Warm the olive oil in a skillet over medium heat. Season the chicken with salt and pepper and cook for 4 minutes on both sides. Stir in garlic, oregano, stock, onion, celery, tomatoes, and olives and bring to a boil. Simmer for 13-15 minutes.

Nutrition Info:
- Info Per Serving: Calories: 140;Fat: 7g;Protein: 11g;Carbs: 13g.

Baked Beef With Kale Slaw & Bell Peppers

Servings:4
Cooking Time:35 Minutes
Ingredients:
- 2 tsp olive oil
- 1 lb skirt steak
- 4 cups kale slaw
- 1 tbsp garlic powder
- Salt and black pepper to taste
- 1 small red onion, sliced
- 10 sundried tomatoes, halved
- ½ red bell pepper, sliced

Directions:
1. Preheat the broiler. Brush steak with olive oil, salt, garlic powder, and pepper and place under the broiler for 10 minutes, turning once. Remove to a cutting board and let rest for 10 minutes, then cut the steak diagonally.
2. In the meantime, place sun-dried tomatoes, kale slaw, onion, and bell pepper in a bowl and mix to combine. Transfer to a serving plate and top with steak slices to serve.

Nutrition Info:
- Info Per Serving: Calories: 359;Fat: 16g;Protein: 38g;Carbs: 22g.

Roasted Pork Tenderloin With Apple Sauce

Servings:4
Cooking Time:35 Minutes
Ingredients:

- 2 tbsp olive oil
- 1 lb pork tenderloin
- Salt and black pepper to taste
- ¼ cup apple jelly
- ¼ cup apple juice
- 2 tbsp wholegrain mustard
- 3 sprigs fresh thyme
- ½ tbsp cornstarch
- ½ tbsp heavy cream

Directions:

1. Preheat oven to 330 F. Warm the oil in a skillet over medium heat. Season the pork with salt and pepper. Sear it for 6-8 minutes on all sides. Transfer to a baking sheet. To the same skillet, add the apple jelly, juice, and mustard and stir for 5 minutes over low heat, stirring often. Top with the pork and thyme sprigs. Place the skillet in the oven and bake for 15-18 minutes, brushing the pork with the apple-mustard sauce every 5 minutes. Remove the pork and let it rest for 15 minutes. Place a small pot over low heat. Blend the cornstarch with heavy cream and cooking juices and pour the mixture into the pot. Stir for 2 minutes until thickens. Drizzle the sauce over the pork. Serve sliced and enjoy!

Nutrition Info:

- Info Per Serving: Calories: 146;Fat: 7g;Protein: 13g;Carbs: 8g.

Turmeric Green Bean & Chicken Bake

Servings:4
Cooking Time:35 Minutes
Ingredients:

- 1 lb green beans, trimmed and halved
- 1 lb chicken thighs, boneless and skinless
- 2 tsp turmeric powder
- ½ cup sour cream
- Salt and black pepper to taste
- 1 tbsp lime juice
- 1 tbsp dill, chopped
- 1 tbsp thyme, chopped

Directions:

1. Preheat the oven to 380 F. Place chicken, turmeric, green beans, sour cream, salt, pepper, lime juice, thyme, and dill in a roasting pan and mix well. Bake for 25 minutes. Serve.

Nutrition Info:

- Info Per Serving: Calories: 280;Fat: 13g;Protein: 15g;Carbs: 21g.

Marjoram Pork Loin With Ricotta Cheese

Servings:4
Cooking Time:70 Minutes
Ingredients:

- 2 tbsp olive oil
- 1 ½ lb pork loin, cubed
- 2 tbsp marjoram, chopped
- 1 garlic clove, minced
- 1 tbsp capers, drained
- 1 cup chicken stock
- Salt and black pepper to taste
- ½ cup ricotta cheese, crumbled

Directions:

1. Warm olive oil in a skillet over medium heat and sear pork for 5 minutes. Stir in marjoram, garlic, capers, stock, salt, and pepper and bring to a boil. Cook for 30 minutes. Mix in cheese.

Nutrition Info:

- Info Per Serving: Calories: 310;Fat: 15g;Protein: 34g;Carbs: 17g.

Mushroom & Pork Stew

Servings: 4
Cooking Time: 8 Hours 10 Minutes

Ingredients:

- 2 tbsp olive oil
- 2 lb pork stew meat, cubed
- 1 lb mushrooms, chopped
- Salt and black pepper to taste
- 2 cups chicken stock
- 1 carrot, chopped
- 1 yellow onion, chopped
- 2 garlic cloves, minced
- 2 cups tomatoes, chopped
- ½ cup parsley, chopped

Directions:

1. Place pork meat, salt, pepper, stock, olive oil, onion, carrot, garlic, mushrooms, and tomatoes in your slow cooker. Cover with the lid and cook for 8 hours on Low. Top with parsley.

Nutrition Info:

- Info Per Serving: Calories: 340;Fat: 18g;Protein: 17g;Carbs: 13g.

Rosemary Spatchcock Chicken

Servings: 6
Cooking Time: 55 Minutes

Ingredients:

- 2 tbsp butter, melted
- 2 tbsp olive oil
- 1 whole chicken
- 8 garlic cloves, chopped
- 2 tbsp rosemary, chopped
- Salt and black pepper to taste
- 2 lemons, thinly sliced

Directions:

1. Preheat oven to 425 F. Put the chicken breast side down on a work surface. With a sharp knife, cut along the backbone, starting at the tail end and working your way up to the neck. Pull apart the two sides, opening up the chicken. Turn it over, breast-side up, pressing down with your hands to flatten the bird. Transfer to a greased baking dish. Loosen the skin over the breasts and thighs by cutting a small incision and sticking one or two fingers inside to pull the skin away from the meat without removing it.
2. In a small bowl, whisk the olive oil, garlic, rosemary, salt, and pepper. Rub the mixture under the skin of each breast and each thigh. Add the lemon slices evenly to the same areas. Mix the melted butter, salt, and pepper and rub over the outside of the chicken. Roast the chicken for 40-45 minutes or until cooked through, and the skin is golden and charred. Leave to rest for 10 minutes, then slice to serve.

Nutrition Info:

- Info Per Serving: Calories: 435;Fat: 34g;Protein: 28g;Carbs: 2g.

Beef Stuffed Peppers

Servings:4
Cooking Time:50 Minutes
Ingredients:
- 2 tbsp olive oil
- 2 red bell peppers
- 1 lb ground beef
- 1 shallot, finely chopped
- 2 garlic cloves, minced
- 2 tbsp fresh sage, chopped
- Salt and black pepper to taste
- 1 tsp ground allspice
- ½ cup fresh parsley, chopped
- ½ cup baby arugula leaves
- ½ cup pine nuts, chopped
- 1 tbsp orange juice

Directions:
1. Warm the olive oil in a large skillet over medium heat. Sauté the beef, garlic, and shallot for 8-10 minutes until the meat is browned and cooked through. Season with sage, allspice, salt, and pepper and remove from the heat to cool slightly. Stir in parsley, arugula, pine nuts, and orange juice and mix.
2. Preheat oven to 390 F. Slice the peppers in half lengthwise and remove the seeds and membranes. Spoon the filling into the pepper halves. Bake the oven for 25-30 minutes.

Nutrition Info:
- Info Per Serving: Calories: 521;Fat: 44g;Protein: 25g;Carbs: 9g.

Valencian Arroz Con Pollo

Servings:4
Cooking Time:40 Minutes
Ingredients:
- 2 tbsp olive oil
- 3 cups chicken stock
- 1 cup brown rice
- 1 tbsp balsamic vinegar
- 1 lb chicken breasts, cubed
- 6 scallions, chopped
- Salt and black pepper to taste
- 1 tbsp sweet paprika
- 1 red bell pepper, chopped
- 1 green bell pepper, chopped

Directions:
1. Warm the olive oil in a skillet over medium heat and cook chicken for 5 minutes, stirring occasionally. Put in scallions and bell peppers and cook for another 5 minutes. Stir in rice, stock, vinegar, salt, pepper, and paprika and bring to a boil. Cook for 20 minutes. Serve immediately.

Nutrition Info:
- Info Per Serving: Calories: 310;Fat: 10g;Protein: 25g;Carbs: 19g.

Juicy Almond Turkey

Servings:4
Cooking Time:40 Minutes
Ingredients:
- 2 tbsp canola oil
- ¼ cup almonds, chopped
- 1 lb turkey breast, sliced
- Salt and black pepper to taste
- 1 lemon, juiced and zested
- 1 grapefruit, juiced
- 1 tbsp rosemary, chopped
- 3 garlic cloves, minced
- 1 cup chicken stock

Directions:
1. Warm the olive oil in a skillet over medium heat and cook garlic and turkey for 8 minutes on both sides. Stir in salt, pepper, lemon juice, lemon zest, grapefruit juice, rosemary, almonds, and stock and bring to a boil. Cook for 20 minutes.

Nutrition Info:
- Info Per Serving: Calories: 300;Fat: 13g;Protein: 25g;Carbs: 19g.

Lamb Kebabs With Lemon-yogurt Sauce

Servings:4
Cooking Time:25 Minutes
Ingredients:
- 2 tbsp olive oil
- 1 lb ground lamb
- 2 tbsp chopped fresh mint
- ¼ cup flour
- ¼ cup chopped red onions
- ¼ cup toasted pine nuts
- 2 tsp ground cumin
- Salt to taste
- 1 tsp ground cinnamon
- ½ tsp ground nutmeg
- ½ tsp black pepper
- 1 cup Greek yogurt
- 1 lemon, zested and juiced

Directions:
1. In a small bowl, whisk the yogurt, olive oil, salt, and lemon zest, and lemon juice. Keep in the refrigerator until ready to serve. Warm the olive oil in a pot over low heat. In a large bowl, combine the lamb, mint, flour, red onions, pine nuts, cumin, salt, cinnamon, ginger, nutmeg, and pepper and mix well with your hands. Shape the mixture into 12 patties. Thread the patties onto skewers and place them on a lined cookie sheet. Set under your preheated broiler for about 12 minutes, flipping once halfway through cooking. Serve the skewers with yogurt sauce.

Nutrition Info:
- Info Per Serving: Calories: 500;Fat: 42g;Protein: 23g;Carbs: 9g.

Holiday Leg Of Lamb

Servings:4
Cooking Time:2 Hours 20 Minutes
Ingredients:
- ½ cup butter
- 2 lb leg of lamb, boneless
- 2 tbsp tomato paste
- 2 tbsp yellow mustard
- 2 tbsp basil, chopped
- 2 garlic cloves, minced
- Salt and black pepper to taste
- 1 cup white wine
- ½ cup sour cream

Directions:
1. Preheat oven to 360 F. Warm butter in a skillet over medium heat. Sear leg of lamb for 10 minutes on all sides. Stir in mustard, basil, tomato paste, garlic, salt, pepper, wine, and sour cream and bake for 2 hours. Serve right away.

Nutrition Info:
- Info Per Serving: Calories: 320;Fat: 13g;Protein: 15g;Carbs: 23g.

Pork Tenderloin With Caraway Seeds

Servings:4
Cooking Time:30 Minutes
Ingredients:

- 2 tbsp olive oil
- 1 lb pork tenderloin, sliced
- Salt and black pepper to taste
- 3 tbsp ground caraway seeds
- 1/3 cup half-and-half
- ½ cup dill, chopped

Directions:

1. Warm the olive oil in a skillet over medium heat and sear pork for 8 minutes on all sides. Stir in salt, pepper, ground caraway seeds, half-and-half, and dill and bring to a boil. Cook for another 12 minutes. Serve warm.

Nutrition Info:

- Info Per Serving: Calories: 330;Fat: 15g;Protein: 18g;Carbs: 15g.

Chicken Tagine With Vegetables

Servings:6
Cooking Time:67 Minutes
Ingredients:

- 1 ½ lb boneless skinless chicken thighs, cut into chunks
- 2 zucchini, sliced into half-moons
- 4 tbsp olive oil
- Salt and black pepper to taste
- 1 small red onion, chopped
- 2 cloves garlic, minced
- 1 red bell pepper, chopped
- 2 tomatoes, chopped
- 1 tbsp harissa paste
- 1 cup water
- 1 cup black olives, halved
- ¼ cup fresh cilantro, chopped

Directions:

1. Warm the olive oil in a large skillet over medium heat. Season the chicken with salt and pepper and brown for 6-8 minutes on all sides. Add the onion, garlic, and bell pepper and sauté for 5 minutes until tender. Stir in harissa paste and tomatoes for 1 minute and pour in 1 cup of water. Bring to a boil and lower the heat to low. Cover and simmer for 35-45 minutes until the chicken is tender and cooked through. Stir in zucchini and olives and continue to cook for 10 minutes until the zucchini is tender. Serve topped with cilantro.

Nutrition Info:

- Info Per Serving: Calories: 358;Fat: 25g;Protein: 25g;Carbs: 8g.

Chicken Meatballs With Peach Topping

Servings: 4
Cooking Time: 25 Minutes

Ingredients:
- 2 tbsp olive oil
- 1 lb ground chicken
- 2 peaches, cubed
- ½ red onion, finely chopped
- 1 lemon, juiced
- 1 garlic clove, minced
- ½ jalapeño pepper, minced
- 2 tbsp chopped fresh cilantro
- Salt and black pepper to taste

Directions:
1. Season the ground chicken with salt and pepper. Shape the mixture into meatballs. Warm olive oil in a pan over medium heat and brown fry the meatballs for 8-10 minutes on all sides until golden brown. In a bowl, combine peaches, lemon juice, garlic, red onion, jalapeño pepper, cilantro, and salt. Top the meatballs with the salsa and serve.

Nutrition Info:
- Info Per Serving: Calories: 312;Fat: 16g;Protein: 33.7g;Carbs: 8g.

Grilled Chicken And Zucchini Kebabs

Servings: 4
Cooking Time: 20 Minutes

Ingredients:
- ¼ cup extra-virgin olive oil
- 2 tablespoons balsamic vinegar
- 1 teaspoon dried oregano, crushed between your fingers
- 1 pound boneless, skinless chicken breasts, cut into 1½-inch pieces
- 2 medium zucchinis, cut into 1-inch pieces
- ½ cup Kalamata olives, pitted and halved
- 2 tablespoons olive brine
- ¼ cup torn fresh basil leaves
- Nonstick cooking spray
- Special Equipment:
- 14 to 15 wooden skewers, soaked for at least 30 minutes

Directions:
1. Spray the grill grates with nonstick cooking spray. Preheat the grill to medium-high heat.
2. In a small bowl, whisk together the olive oil, vinegar, and oregano. Divide the marinade between two large plastic zip-top bags
3. Add the chicken to one bag and the zucchini to another. Seal and massage the marinade into both the chicken and zucchini.
4. Thread the chicken onto 6 wooden skewers. Thread the zucchini onto 8 or 9 wooden skewers.
5. Cook the kebabs in batches on the grill for 5 minutes, flip, and grill for 5 minutes more, or until any chicken juices run clear.
6. Remove the chicken and zucchini from the skewers to a large serving bowl. Toss with the olives, olive brine, and basil and serve.

Nutrition Info:
- Info Per Serving: Calories: 283;Fat: 15.0g;Protein: 11.0g;Carbs: 26.0g.

Original Meatballs

Servings: 4
Cooking Time: 25 Minutes

Ingredients:
- 2 tbsp olive oil
- 1 lb ground beef meat
- 1 onion, chopped
- 3 tbsp cilantro, chopped
- 1 garlic clove, minced
- Salt and black pepper to taste

Directions:
1. Combine beef, onion, cilantro, garlic, salt, and pepper in a bowl and form meatballs out of the mixture. Sprinkle with oil. Preheat the grill over medium heat and grill them for 14 minutes on all sides. Serve with salad.

Nutrition Info:
- Info Per Serving: Calories: 240; Fat: 15g; Protein: 13g; Carbs: 17g.

Baked Teriyaki Turkey Meatballs

Servings: 6
Cooking Time: 20 Minutes

Ingredients:
- 1 pound lean ground turkey
- 1 egg, whisked
- ¼ cup finely chopped scallions, both white and green parts
- 2 garlic cloves, minced
- 2 tablespoons reduced-sodium tamari or gluten-free soy sauce
- 1 teaspoon grated fresh ginger
- 1 tablespoon honey
- 2 teaspoons mirin
- 1 teaspoon olive oil

Directions:
1. Preheat the oven to 400ºF. Line a baking sheet with parchment paper and set aside.
2. Mix together the ground turkey, whisked egg, scallions, garlic, tamari, ginger, honey, mirin, and olive oil in a large bowl, and stir until well blended.
3. Using a tablespoon to scoop out rounded heaps of the turkey mixture, and then roll them into balls with your hands. Transfer the balls to the prepared baking sheet.
4. Bake in the preheated oven for 20 minutes, flipping the balls with a spatula halfway through, or until the meatballs are browned and cooked through.
5. Serve warm.

Nutrition Info:
- Info Per Serving: Calories: 158; Fat: 8.6g; Protein: 16.2g; Carbs: 4.0g.

Pork Chops In Tomato Olive Sauce

Servings:4
Cooking Time:20 Minutes
Ingredients:
- 2 tbsp olive oil
- 4 pork loin chops, boneless
- 6 tomatoes, crushed
- 3 tbsp basil, chopped
- 10 black olives, halved
- 1 yellow onion, chopped
- 1 garlic clove, minced

Directions:
1. Warm the olive oil in a skillet over medium heat and brown pork chops for 6 minutes on all sides. Share into plates. In the same skillet, stir tomatoes, basil, olives, onion, and garlic and simmer for 4 minutes. Drizzle tomato sauce over.

Nutrition Info:
- Info Per Serving: Calories: 340;Fat: 18g;Protein: 35g;Carbs: 13g.

One-pan Turkish Turkey

Servings:4
Cooking Time:35 Minutes
Ingredients:
- 1 tbsp sunflower seeds, toasted
- 3 tbsp avocado oil
- 1 turkey breast, sliced
- 1 ¼ cups chicken stock
- Salt and black pepper to taste
- ¼ cup parsley, chopped
- 4 oz feta cheese, crumbled
- ¼ cup red onion, chopped
- 1 tbsp lemon juice

Directions:
1. Warm the avocado oil in a skillet over medium heat and sear turkey for 8 minutes on both sides. Mix in stock, salt, pepper, parsley, onion, and lemon juice and bring to a boil. Cook for 15 minutes. Remove to a serving plate and top with feta cheese and sunflower seeds to serve.

Nutrition Info:
- Info Per Serving: Calories: 290;Fat: 15g;Protein: 26g;Carbs: 20g.

Fruits, Desserts And Snacks Recipes

Roasted Eggplant Hummus

Servings:4
Cooking Time:25 Minutes
Ingredients:
- 1 lb eggplants, peeled and sliced
- 1 lemon, juiced
- 1 garlic clove, minced
- ¼ cup tahini
- ¼ tsp ground cumin
- Salt and black pepper to taste
- 2 tbsp fresh parsley, chopped
- ½ cup mayonnaise

Directions:
1. Preheat oven to 350 F. Arrange the eggplant slices on a baking sheet and bake for 15 minutes until tender. Let cool slightly before chopping. In a food processor, mix eggplants, salt, lemon juice, tahini, cumin, garlic, and pepper for 30 seconds. Remove to a bowl. Stir in mayonnaise. Serve topped with parsley.

Nutrition Info:
- Info Per Serving: Calories: 235;Fat: 18g;Protein: 4.1g;Carbs: 17g.

Artichoke & Curly Kale Flatbread

Servings:4
Cooking Time:25 Minutes
Ingredients:
- 3 tbsp olive oil
- 1 cup curly kale, chopped
- 1 tbsp garlic powder
- 2 tbsp parsley, chopped
- 2 flatbread wraps
- 4 tbsp Parmesan cheese, grated
- ½ cup mozzarella, grated
- 14 oz canned artichokes
- 12 cherry tomatoes, halved
- Salt and black pepper to taste

Directions:
1. Preheat the oven to 390 F. Line a baking sheet with parchment paper. Brush the flatbread wrap with some olive oil and sprinkle with garlic, salt, and pepper. Top with half of the Parmesan and mozzarella cheeses. Combine artichokes, tomatoes, salt, pepper, and remaining olive oil in a bowl. Spread the mixture on the top of the wraps and top with the remaining Parmesan cheese. Transfer to the baking sheet and bake for 15 minutes. Top with curly kale and parsley.

Nutrition Info:
- Info Per Serving: Calories: 230;Fat: 12g;Protein: 8g;Carbs: 16g.

Speedy Cucumber Canapes

Servings:4
Cooking Time:5 Minutes
Ingredients:
- 2 tbsp olive oil
- 2 cucumbers, sliced into rounds
- 12 cherry tomatoes, halved
- Salt and black pepper to taste
- 1 red chili pepper, dried
- 8 oz cream cheese, softened
- 1 tbsp balsamic vinegar
- 1 tsp chives, chopped

Directions:
1. In a bowl, mix cream cheese, balsamic vinegar, olive oil, chili pepper, and chives. Season with salt and pepper. Spread the mixture over the cucumber rounds and top with the cherry tomato halves. Serve.

Nutrition Info:
- Info Per Serving: Calories: 130;Fat: 3g;Protein: 3g;Carbs: 7g.

Basic Pudding With Kiwi

Servings:4
Cooking Time:20 Min + Chilling Time
Ingredients:
- 2 kiwi, peeled and sliced
- 1 egg
- 2 ¼ cups milk
- ½ cup honey
- 1 tsp vanilla extract
- 3 tbsp cornstarch

Directions:
1. In a bowl, beat the egg with honey. Stir in 2 cups of milk and vanilla. Pour into a pot over medium heat and bring to a boil. Combine cornstarch and remaining milk in a bowl. Pour slowly into the pot and boil for 1 minute until thickened, stirring often. Divide between 4 cups and transfer to the fridge. Top with kiwi and serve.

Nutrition Info:
- Info Per Serving: Calories: 262;Fat: 4.1g;Protein: 6.5g;Carbs: 52g.

Iberian Spread For Sandwiches

Servings:4
Cooking Time:10 Minutes
Ingredients:
- 16 pimiento stuffed manzanilla olives
- 4 oz roasted pimientos
- 2/3 cup aioli

Directions:
1. Place the olives and roasted pimientos in your food processor. Pulse until a creamier consistency is formed. Transfer to a bowl and mix well with aioli. Serve and enjoy!

Nutrition Info:
- Info Per Serving: Calories: 325;Fat: 34g;Protein: 0.1g;Carbs: 2g.

Cheese Stuffed Potato Skins

Servings:4
Cooking Time:40 Minutes
Ingredients:
- 2 tbsp olive oil
- 1 lb red baby potatoes
- 1 cup ricotta cheese, crumbled
- 2 garlic cloves, minced
- 1 tbsp chives, chopped
- ½ tsp hot chili sauce
- Salt and black pepper to taste

Directions:
1. Place potatoes and enough water in a pot over medium heat and bring to a boil. Simmer for 15 minutes and drain. Let them cool. Cut them in halves and scoop out the pulp. Place the pulp in a bowl and mash it a bit with a fork. Add in the ricotta cheese, olive oil, garlic, chives, chili sauce, salt, and pepper. Mix to combine. Fill potato skins with the mixture.
2. Preheat oven to 360 F. Line a baking sheet with parchment paper. Place filled skins on the sheet and bake for 10 minutes.

Nutrition Info:
- Info Per Serving: Calories: 310;Fat: 10g;Protein: 9g;Carbs: 23g.

Spicy Roasted Chickpeas

Servings:2
Cooking Time:40 Minutes
Ingredients:
- Chickpeas
- 1 tbsp olive oil
- 1 can chickpeas
- Salt to taste
- Seasoning Mix
- ¾ tsp cumin
- ½ tsp ground coriander
- Salt and black pepper to taste
- ¼ tsp chili powder
- ½ tsp cayenne pepper
- ¼ tsp cardamom
- ¼ tsp cinnamon
- ¼ tsp allspice

Directions:
1. Preheat oven to 400 F. In a small bowl, place all the seasoning mix ingredients and stir well to combine.
2. Place the chickpeas in a bowl and season them with olive oil and salt. Add the chickpeas to a lined baking sheet and roast them for about 25-35 minutes, turning them over once or twice while cooking until they are slightly crisp. Remove to a bowl and sprinkle them with the seasoning mix. Toss lightly to combine. Serve and enjoy!

Nutrition Info:
- Info Per Serving: Calories: 268;Fat: 11g;Protein: 11g;Carbs: 35g.

Garbanzo Patties With Cilantro-yogurt Sauce

Servings:4
Cooking Time:20 Minutes
Ingredients:
- ¼ cup olive oil
- 3 garlic cloves, minced
- 1 cup canned garbanzo beans
- 2 tbsp parsley, chopped
- 1 onion, chopped
- 1 tsp ground coriander
- Salt and black pepper to taste
- ¼ tsp cayenne pepper
- ¼ tsp cumin powder
- 1 tsp lemon juice
- 3 tbsp flour
- ¼ cup Greek yogurt
- 2 tbsp chopped cilantro
- ½ tsp garlic powder

Directions:
1. In a blender, blitz garbanzo, parsley, onion, garlic, salt, pepper, ground coriander, cayenne pepper, cumin powder, and lemon juice until smooth. Remove to a bowl and mix in flour. Form 16 balls out of the mixture and flatten them into patties.
2. Warm the olive oil in a skillet over medium heat and fry patties for 10 minutes on both sides. Remove them to a paper towel–lined plate to drain the excess fat. In a bowl, mix the Greek yogurt, cilantro, garlic powder, salt, and pepper. Serve the patties with yogurt sauce.

Nutrition Info:
- Info Per Serving: Calories: 120;Fat: 7g;Protein: 4g;Carbs: 13g.

Tuna, Tomato & Burrata Salad

Servings:4
Cooking Time:10 Minutes
Ingredients:
- 2 tbsp extra-virgin olive oil
- 2 tbsp canned tuna, flaked
- 4 heirloom tomato slices
- Salt and black pepper to taste
- 4 burrata cheese slices
- 8 fresh basil leaves, sliced
- 1 tbsp balsamic vinegar

Directions:
1. Place the tomatoes on a plate. Top with burrata slices and tuna. Sprinkle with basil. Drizzle with olive oil and balsamic vinegar and serve.

Nutrition Info:
- Info Per Serving: Calories: 153;Fat: 13g;Protein: 7g;Carbs: 2g.

White Bean Dip With Pita Wedges

Servings:4
Cooking Time:25 Minutes
Ingredients:
- ½ cup olive oil
- 1 garlic clove
- 1 can cannellini beans
- 1 lemon, zested and juiced
- Salt to taste
- ½ tsp oregano
- 4 pitas, cut into wedges
- 5 black olives

Directions:
1. Preheat the oven to 350 F. Arrange the pita wedges on a baking sheet and sprinkle with salt and oregano; drizzle them with some olive oil. Bake for 10-12 minutes until the pita beginning to brown. Place the beans, garlic, lemon juice, lemon zest, and salt and purée, drizzling in as much olive oil as needed until the beans are smooth. Transfer the dip to a bowl and serve the toasted pita bread.

Nutrition Info:
- Info Per Serving: Calories: 209;Fat: 17g;Protein: 4g;Carbs: 12g.

Sicilian Almond Granita

Servings:4
Cooking Time:5 Min + Freezing Time
Ingredients:
- 4 small oranges, chopped
- ½ tsp almond extract
- 2 tbsp lemon juice
- 1 cup orange juice
- ¼ cup honey
- Fresh mint leaves for garnish

Directions:
1. In a food processor, mix oranges, orange juice, honey, almond extract, and lemon juice. Pulse until smooth. Pour in a dip dish and freeze for 1 hour. Mix with a fork and freeze for 30 minutes more. Repeat a couple of times. Pour into dessert glasses and garnish with basil leaves. Serve.

Nutrition Info:
- Info Per Serving: Calories: 145;Fat: 0g;Protein: 1.5g;Carbs: 36g.

Pepperoni Fat Head Pizza

Servings:4
Cooking Time:35 Minutes
Ingredients:
- 2 tbsp olive oil
- 2 cups flour
- 1 cup lukewarm water
- 1 pinch of sugar
- 1 tsp active dry yeast
- ¾ tsp salt
- 1 tsp dried oregano
- 2 cups mozzarella cheese
- 1 cup sliced pepperoni

Directions:
1. Sift the flour and salt in a bowl and stir in yeast. Mix lukewarm water, olive oil, and sugar in another bowl. Add the wet mixture to the dry mixture and whisk until you obtain a soft dough. Place the dough on a lightly floured work surface and knead it thoroughly for 4-5 minutes until elastic. Transfer the dough to a greased bowl. Cover with cling film and leave to rise for 50-60 minutes in a warm place until doubled in size. Roll out the dough to a thickness of around 12 inches.
2. Preheat oven to 400 F. Line a round pizza pan with parchment paper. Spread the dough on the pizza pan and top with the mozzarella cheese, oregano, and pepperoni slices. Bake in the oven for 15 minutes or until the cheese melts. Remove the pizza from the oven and let cool slightly. Slice and serve.

Nutrition Info:
- Info Per Serving: Calories: 229;Fat: 7g;Protein: 36g;Carbs: 0.4g.

Berry And Rhubarb Cobbler

Servings:8
Cooking Time: 35 Minutes
Ingredients:
- Cobbler:
- 1 cup fresh raspberries
- 2 cups fresh blueberries
- 1 cup sliced (½-inch) rhubarb pieces
- 1 tablespoon arrowroot powder
- ¼ cup unsweetened apple juice
- 2 tablespoons melted coconut oil
- ¼ cup raw honey
- Topping:
- 1 cup almond flour
- 1 tablespoon arrowroot powder
- ½ cup shredded coconut
- ¼ cup raw honey
- ½ cup coconut oil

Directions:
1. Make the Cobbler
2. Preheat the oven to 350ºF. Grease a baking dish with melted coconut oil.
3. Combine the ingredients for the cobbler in a large bowl. Stir to mix well.
4. Spread the mixture in the single layer on the baking dish. Set aside.
5. Make the Topping
6. Combine the almond flour, arrowroot powder, and coconut in a bowl. Stir to mix well.
7. Fold in the honey and coconut oil. Stir with a fork until the mixture crumbled.
8. Spread the topping over the cobbler, then bake in the preheated oven for 35 minutes or until frothy and golden brown.
9. Serve immediately.

Nutrition Info:
- Info Per Serving: Calories: 305;Fat: 22.1g;Protein: 3.2g;Carbs: 29.8g.

Homemade Studentenfutter

Servings:4
Cooking Time:10 Minutes
Ingredients:
- ¼ cup dried figs
- ½ cup almonds
- ¼ seed mix
- ¼ cup dried cranberries
- ½ cup walnut halves
- ½ cup hazelnuts
- ½ tsp paprika
- 1 tbsp Parmesan cheese, grated

Directions:
1. Spread the almonds, walnuts, hazelnuts, and seeds on a greased baking dish. Bake in preheated oven for 10 minutes at 350 F. Remove and mix with figs and cranberries. Toss to combine. Sprinkle with Parmesan and paprika and serve.

Nutrition Info:
- Info Per Serving: Calories: 195;Fat: 15.6g;Protein: 7g;Carbs: 9.8g.

Home-style Trail Mix

Servings: 4
Cooking Time: 30 Minutes

Ingredients:
- 1 cup dried apricots, cut into thin strips
- 2 tbsp olive oil
- 1 cup pepitas
- 1 cup walnut halves
- 1 cup dried dates, chopped
- 1 cup golden raisins
- 1 cup raw almonds
- 1 tsp salt

Directions:
1. Preheat the oven to 310 F. Combine almonds, pepitas, dates, walnuts, apricots, and raisins in a bowl. Mix in olive oil and salt and toss to coat. Spread the mixture on a lined with parchment paper sheet, and bake for 30 minutes or until the fruits are slightly browned. Let to cool before serving.

Nutrition Info:
- Info Per Serving: Calories: 267;Fat: 14g;Protein: 7g;Carbs: 35g.

Fig & Mascarpone Toasts With Pistachios

Servings: 6
Cooking Time: 10 Minutes

Ingredients:
- 4 tbsp butter, melted
- 1 French baguette, sliced
- 1 cup Mascarpone cheese
- 1 jar fig jam
- ½ cup crushed pistachios

Directions:
1. Preheat oven to 350 F. Arrange the sliced bread on a greased baking sheet and brush each slice with melted butter.
2. Toast the bread for 5-7 minutes until golden brown. Let the bread cool slightly. Spread about a teaspoon of the mascarpone cheese on each piece of bread. Top with fig jam and pistachios.

Nutrition Info:
- Info Per Serving: Calories: 445;Fat: 24g;Protein: 3g;Carbs: 48g.

Coconut Blueberries With Brown Rice

Servings: 4
Cooking Time: 10 Minutes

Ingredients:
- 1 cup fresh blueberries
- 2 cups unsweetened coconut milk
- 1 teaspoon ground ginger
- ¼ cup maple syrup
- Sea salt, to taste
- 2 cups cooked brown rice

Directions:
1. Put all the ingredients, except for the brown rice, in a pot. Stir to combine well.
2. Cook over medium-high heat for 7 minutes or until the blueberries are tender.
3. Pour in the brown rice and cook for 3 more minute or until the rice is soft. Stir constantly.
4. Serve immediately.

Nutrition Info:
- Info Per Serving: Calories: 470;Fat: 24.8g;Protein: 6.2g;Carbs: 60.1g.

Authentic Greek Potato Skins

Servings: 4
Cooking Time: 1 Hour 10 Minutes
Ingredients:
- 2 tbsp extra-virgin olive oil
- 1 cup feta cheese, crumbled
- 1 lb potatoes
- ½ cup Greek yogurt
- 2 spring onions, chopped
- 3 sundried tomatoes, chopped
- 6 Kalamata olives, chopped
- ½ tsp dried dill
- 1 tsp Greek oregano
- 2 tbsp halloumi cheese, grated
- Salt and black pepper to taste

Directions:
1. Preheat oven to 400 F. Pierce the potatoes in several places with a fork. Wrap in aluminum foil and bake in the oven for 45-50 minutes until tender. Let cool. Split the cooled potatoes lengthwise and scoop out some of the flesh. Put the flesh in a bowl and mash with a fork.
2. Add in the spring onions, sun-dried tomatoes, olives, dill, oregano, feta cheese, and yogurt and stir. Season with salt and pepper. Fill the potato shells with the feta mixture and top with halloumi cheese. Transfer the boats to a baking sheet and place under the broiler for 5 minutes until the top is golden and crisp. Serve right away.

Nutrition Info:
- Info Per Serving: Calories: 294;Fat: 18g;Protein: 12g;Carbs: 22g.

Amaretto Nut Bars

Servings: 4
Cooking Time: 10 Minutes
Ingredients:
- 2 tbsp olive oil
- ¼ cup shredded coconut
- 1 cup pistachios
- ½ tsp Amaretto liqueur
- 1 cup almonds
- 2 cups dates, pitted
- ¼ cup cocoa powder

Directions:
1. In a food processor, blend pistachios, dates, almonds, olive oil, Amaretto liqueur, and cocoa powder until well minced. Make tablespoon-size balls out of the mixture. Roll the balls in the shredded coconut to coat. Serve chilled.

Nutrition Info:
- Info Per Serving: Calories: 560;Fat: 28g;Protein: 11g;Carbs: 79g.

Quick & Easy Red Dip

Servings: 4
Cooking Time: 10 Minutes
Ingredients:
- 1 cup roasted red peppers, chopped
- 3 tbsp olive oil
- 1 lb tomatoes, chopped
- Salt and black pepper to taste
- 1 ½ tsp balsamic vinegar
- ½ tsp oregano, chopped
- 2 garlic cloves, minced
- 2 tbsp parsley, chopped

Directions:
1. In a food processor, blend tomatoes, red peppers, salt, pepper, vinegar, oregano, olive oil, garlic, and parsley until smooth. Store this in the fridge for a few days, up to a week.

Nutrition Info:
- Info Per Serving: Calories: 130;Fat: 5g;Protein: 4g;Carbs: 4g.

Apple And Berries Ambrosia

Servings:4
Cooking Time: 0 Minutes
Ingredients:
- 2 cups unsweetened coconut milk, chilled
- 2 tablespoons raw honey
- 1 apple, peeled, cored, and chopped
- 2 cups fresh raspberries
- 2 cups fresh blueberries

Directions:
1. Spoon the chilled milk in a large bowl, then mix in the honey. Stir to mix well.
2. Then mix in the remaining ingredients. Stir to coat the fruits well and serve immediately.

Nutrition Info:
- Info Per Serving: Calories: 386;Fat: 21.1g;Protein: 4.2g;Carbs: 45.9g.

Pecan & Raspberry & Frozen Yogurt Cups

Servings:4
Cooking Time:10 Minutes
Ingredients:
- 2 cups fresh raspberries
- 4 cups vanilla frozen yogurt
- 1 lime, zested
- ¼ cup chopped praline pecans

Directions:
1. Divide the frozen yogurt into 4 dessert glasses. Top with raspberries, lime zest, and pecans. Serve immediately.

Nutrition Info:
- Info Per Serving: Calories: 142;Fat: 3.4g;Protein: 3.7g;Carbs: 26g.

Portuguese Orange Mug Cake

Servings:2
Cooking Time:12 Minutes
Ingredients:
- 2 tbsp butter, melted
- 6 tbsp flour
- 2 tbsp sugar
- ½ tsp baking powder
- ¼ tsp salt
- 1 tsp orange zest
- 1 egg
- 2 tbsp orange juice
- 2 tbsp milk
- ½ tsp orange extract
- ½ tsp vanilla extract
- Orange slices for garnish

Directions:
1. In a bowl, beat the egg, butter, orange juice, milk, orange extract, and vanilla extract. In another bowl, combine the flour, sugar, baking powder, salt, and orange zest. Pour the dry ingredients into the wet ingredients and stir to combine. Spoon the mixture into 2 mugs and microwave one at a time for 1-2 minutes. Garnish with orange slices.

Nutrition Info:
- Info Per Serving: Calories: 302;Fat: 17g;Protein: 6g;Carbs: 33g.

Cinnamon Pear & Oat Crisp With Pecans

Servings: 4
Cooking Time: 30 Minutes
Ingredients:
- 2 tbsp butter, melted
- 4 fresh pears, mashed
- ½ lemon, juiced and zested
- ¼ cup maple syrup
- 1 cup gluten-free rolled oats
- ½ cup chopped pecans
- ½ tsp ground cinnamon
- ¼ tsp salt

Directions:
1. Preheat oven to 350 F. Combine the pears, lemon juice and zest, and maple syrup in a bowl. Stir to mix well, then spread the mixture on a greased baking dish. Combine the remaining ingredients in a small bowl. Stir to mix well. Pour the mixture over the pear mixture. Bake for 20 minutes or until the oats are golden brown.

Nutrition Info:
- Info Per Serving: Calories: 496; Fat: 33g; Protein: 5g; Carbs: 50.8g.

Dates Stuffed With Mascarpone & Almonds

Servings: 6
Cooking Time: 10 Minutes
Ingredients:
- 20 blanched almonds
- 8 oz mascarpone cheese
- 20 Medjool dates
- 2 tbsp honey

Directions:
1. Using a knife, cut one side of the date lengthwise from the stem to the bottom. Gently remove the stone and replace it with a blanched almond. Spoon the cheese into a piping bag. Squeeze a generous amount of the cheese into each date. Set the dates on a serving plate and drizzle with honey. Serve immediately or chill in the fridge.

Nutrition Info:
- Info Per Serving: Calories: 253; Fat: 15g; Protein: 2g; Carbs: 31g.

Chocolate And Avocado Mousse

Servings: 4
Cooking Time: 5 Minutes
Ingredients:
- 8 ounces dark chocolate, chopped
- ¼ cup unsweetened coconut milk
- 2 tablespoons coconut oil
- 2 ripe avocados, deseeded
- ¼ cup raw honey
- Sea salt, to taste

Directions:
1. Put the chocolate in a saucepan. Pour in the coconut milk and add the coconut oil.
2. Cook for 3 minutes or until the chocolate and coconut oil melt. Stir constantly.
3. Put the avocado in a food processor, then drizzle with honey and melted chocolate. Pulse to combine until smooth.
4. Pour the mixture in a serving bowl, then sprinkle with salt. Refrigerate to chill for 30 minutes and serve.

Nutrition Info:
- Info Per Serving: Calories: 654; Fat: 46.8g; Protein: 7.2g; Carbs: 55.9g.

Appendix : Recipes Index

A

Almond-cherry Oatmeal Bowls 6
Amaretto Nut Bars 83
Apple & Date Smoothie 8
Apple And Berries Ambrosia 84
Apricot Chicken Rice Bowls 66
Artichoke & Bean Pot 52
Artichoke & Curly Kale Flatbread 76
Arugula & Caper Green Salad 43
Arugula & Fruit Salad 47
Asparagus & Goat Cheese Rice Salad 26
Authentic Greek Potato Skins 83
Autumn Vegetable & Rigatoni Bake 22
Avocado Shrimp Ceviche 30

B

Baked Beef With Kale Slaw & Bell Peppers 67
Baked Cod With Vegetables 37
Baked Halibut Steaks With Vegetables 32
Baked Potato With Veggie Mix 54
Baked Salmon With Tarragon Mustard Sauce 31
Baked Teriyaki Turkey Meatballs 74
Banana & Chocolate Porridge 11
Basic Pudding With Kiwi 77
Basil Scrambled Eggs 16
Bean & Squash Soup 50
Bean And Veggie Pasta 29
Beef Stuffed Peppers 70
Bell Pepper & Roasted Cabbage Salad 46
Berry And Rhubarb Cobbler 81
Black Bean & Chickpea Burgers 20
Brussels Sprouts Linguine 52

C

Cabbage & Turkey Soup 51
Calamari In Garlic-cilantro Sauce 33
Caper & Herring Stuffed Eggs 33
Carrot & Caper Chickpeas 28
Cauliflower Cakes With Goat Cheese 62
Cauliflower Hash With Carrots 56
Cauliflower Rice Risotto With Mushrooms 57
Celery And Mustard Greens 60
Chargrilled Vegetable Kebabs 59
Cheese & Pecan Salad With Orange Dressing 50

Cheese Stuffed Potato Skins 78
Cheesy Smoked Salmon Crostini 36
Cherry Tomato & Mushroom Frittata 14
Cherry, Apricot, And Pecan Brown Rice Bowl 25
Chia & Almond Oatmeal 9
Chicken Meatballs With Peach Topping 73
Chicken Sausage & Zucchini Soup 65
Chicken Tagine With Vegetables 72
Chicken Thighs With Roasted Artichokes 65
Chickpea Lettuce Wraps With Celery 57
Chili Lentil Soup 42
Chili Pork Rice 27
Chili Vegetable Skillet 56
Chocolate And Avocado Mousse 85
Chocolate-strawberry Smoothie 10
Cinnamon Pear & Oat Crisp With Pecans 85
Coconut Blueberries With Brown Rice 82
Cod Fillets In Mushroom Sauce 31
Collard Green & Rice Salad 43
Corn & Cucumber Salad 45
Crab Stuffed Celery Sticks 30
Creamy Asparagus & Parmesan Linguine 24
Creamy Shrimp With Tie Pasta 27
Crustless Tiropita (greek Cheese Pie) 15
Cucumber & Spelt Salad With Chicken 41

D

Dates Stuffed With Mascarpone & Almonds 85
Dill Chutney Salmon 36
Dilly Salmon Frittata 7
Drunken Mussels With Lemon-butter Sauce 38

E

Easy Alfalfa Sprout And Nut Rolls 17
Easy Zucchini Patties 60
Egg Bake 15
Eggplant Rolls In Tomato Sauce 58
Energy Nut Smoothie 16

F

Feta & Cannellini Bean Soup 45
Fig & Mascarpone Toasts With Pistachios 82
Fofu Spaghetti Bolognese 21
Fruit Salad With Sesame Seeds & Nuts 49

G

Garbanzo Patties With Cilantro-yogurt Sauce 79
Garlic Shrimp With Arugula Pesto 40

Garlic Shrimp With Mushrooms 40
Garlicky Broccoli Rabe 57
Grilled Chicken And Zucchini Kebabs 73
Grilled Eggplant "steaks" With Sauce 62
Grilled Lemon Pesto Salmon 33
Grilled Vegetable Skewers 55
Grilled Za´atar Zucchini Rounds 55

H

Hearty Butternut Spinach, And Cheeses Lasagna 29
Herby Beef Soup 64
Herby Cod Skewers 38
Herby Yogurt Sauce 46
Holiday Leg Of Lamb 71
Homemade Studentenfutter 81
Homemade Vegetarian Moussaka 61
Home-style Trail Mix 82
Honey & Feta Frozen Yogurt 13

I

Iberian Spread For Sandwiches 77
Italian Hot Green Beans 59
Italian Pork Meatball Soup 47

J

Juicy Almond Turkey 71

K

Kale And Apple Smoothie 13

L

Lamb Kebabs With Lemon-yogurt Sauce 71
Leek & Olive Cod Casserole 32
Leek Cream Soup With Hazelnuts 47
Lemon-basil Spaghetti 28
Lemony Sea Bass 35
Lemony Tuna Barley With Capers 19

M

Mango-yogurt Smoothie 12
Maple Berry & Walnut Oatmeal 13
Marjoram Pork Loin With Ricotta Cheese 68
Minty Bulgur With Fried Halloumi 48
Mushroom & Green Onion Rice Pilaf 22
Mushroom & Pork Stew 69
Mushroom And Caramelized Onion Musakhan 9

Mushroom And Soba Noodle Soup 48
Mushroom Chicken Piccata 66

O

One-pan Turkish Turkey 75
One-skillet Salmon With Olives & Escarole 37
Original Meatballs 74

P

Pan-seared Trout With Tzatziki 38
Paprika Spinach & Chickpea Bowl 25
Parchment Orange & Dill Salmon 39
Parmesan Oatmeal With Greens 6
Pea & Carrot Noodles 61
Pecan & Raspberry & Frozen Yogurt Cups 84
Pepperoni Fat Head Pizza 80
Picante Avocado Salad With Anchovies 51
Pork Chops In Tomato Olive Sauce 75
Pork Tenderloin With Caraway Seeds 72
Portuguese Orange Mug Cake 84
Pumpkin-yogurt Parfaits 11

Q

Quick & Easy Bread In A Mug 11
Quick & Easy Red Dip 83

R

Ratatouille 63
Red Pepper Coques With Pine Nuts 7
Ritzy Summer Fruit Salad 42
Roasted Cod With Cabbage 36
Roasted Eggplant Hummus 76
Roasted Pork Tenderloin With Apple Sauce 68
Roasted Vegetable Medley 58
Roasted Vegetable Panini 10
Root Vegetable Roast 43
Rosemary Barley With Walnuts 20
Rosemary Pork Chops With Cabbage Mix 64
Rosemary Spatchcock Chicken 69
Rosemary Wine Poached Haddock 39

S

Sautéed Kale With Olives 49
Savory Breakfast Oatmeal 14
Seafood Stew 34
Seared Halibut With Moroccan Chermoula 34
Sicilian Almond Granita 80

Simple Green Rice 24
Simple Oven-baked Green Beans 60
Simple Tuna Salad 46
Slow Cooked Turkey And Brown Rice 23
Slow Cooker Pork & Bean Cassoulet 18
Smoky Paprika Chickpeas 19
Sole Piccata With Capers 39
Spanish Chicken Skillet 67
Speedy Cucumber Canapes 77
Spicy Grilled Shrimp With Lemon Wedges 35
Spicy Kale With Almonds 53
Spicy Roasted Chickpeas 78
Spicy Tofu Tacos With Cherry Tomato Salsa 8
Spinach & Chickpea Soup With Sausages 44
Sumptuous Greek Vegetable Salad 41
Swiss Chard Couscous With Feta Cheese 19
Swoodles With Almond Butter Sauce 26

T

Tahini & Feta Butternut Squash 63
Tomato And Egg Scramble 17
Tri-color Salad 44
Tuna, Tomato & Burrata Salad 79
Turkish-style Orzo 22
Turmeric Green Bean & Chicken Bake 68
Two-bean Cassoulet 21

V

Valencian Arroz Con Pollo 70
Vegetable Quinoa & Garbanzo Skillet 23
Veggie & Egg Quinoa With Pancetta 18
Veggie Rice Bowls With Pesto Sauce 53
Veggie-stuffed Portabello Mushrooms 54

W

White Bean Dip With Pita Wedges 79
White Pizzas With Arugula And Spinach 12

Z

Zesty Asparagus Salad 44

Printed in Great Britain
by Amazon